A SIMPLY BEAUTIFUL WEDDING

EILEEN SILVA KINDIG

InterVarsity Press
Downers Grove, Illinois

InterVarsity Press
P.O. Box 1400, Downers Grove, IL 60515
World Wide Web. www ivpress com
E-mail mail@ivpress com

InterVarsity Press® is the book-publishing division of InterVarsity Christian Fellowship/USA®, a
student movement active on campus at hundreds of universities, colleges and schools of nursing in
the United States of America, and a member movement of the International Fellowship of
Evangelical Students. For information about local and regional activities, write Public Relations
Dept, InterVarsity Christian Fellowship/USA, 6400 Schroeder Rd, P.O. Box 7895, Madison, WI
53707-7895

Scripture quotations, unless otherwise noted, are from the Revised Standard Version of the Bible,
copyright 1946, 1952, 1971 by the Division of Christian Education of the National Council of the
Churches of Christ in the USA Used by permission

Cover photograph SuperStock

ISBN 0-8308-1923-1

Printed in the United States of America ♽

Library of Congress Cataloging-in-Publication Data

Kindig, Eileen Silva
  A simply beautiful wedding / Eileen Silva Kindig
   p cm
  Includes bibliographical references
  ISBN 0-8308-1923-1
  1 Weddings—United States—Planning 2 Stress (Psychology)
  3. Simplicity 4. Marriage—Religious aspects—Christianity
  I. Title
  HQ745 K46 1999
  395.2'2—dc21
                                           99-15063
                                              CIP

16	15	14	13	12	11	10	9	8	7	6	5	4	3	2	1
11	10	09	08	07	06	05	04	03	02	01	00	99			

For my dear friend Elizabeth Nelson.
This one's for you, kid—
you more than earned it!

CONTENTS

Acknowledgments

There's nothing like an engagement in the family to teach you everything you ever wanted to know about weddings but were afraid to ask! My deepest appreciation goes to my daughter Moira and my son-in-law Brian for the crash course they gave me in Wedding 101. I am also thankful to the entire Watson family—Mary, Harry, Jeff and Julie—for proving that it's possible to put the Simply Beautiful tenets into practice with heart-warming results.

Thanks, too, to my weekly writers' group—Dandi Mackall, Laura Williams, Laurie Knowleton, Nancy Peacock and Norma Kelly—for listening ad nauseum to these pages and to my California writer friends, Stephanie Gordon and Judy Enderle, for suffering through several chapters during their annual trip to Ohio. I love you guys!

Without Mary and Aaron Olson and Mary's mom, Helen Mutzabaugh, there would have been no chapter ten. Words cannot express how much I appreciated being welcomed into the heart of a precious family moment. All those hours over coffee at Arabica were not only enlightening but fun!

As for my beloved librarians at the Medina County District Library, 1998 winner of the American Library Association Best Library in the nation award, wherever can I find a thank you large enough to encompass you all? I don't think it's possible, but I have to try. Liz Nelson, Barb Chase, Kathy Petras, Mary Olson, Pat Hurd, Anne Hamrick, Tammy Daubner and Renee Dunn spent hours digging through the stacks, ordering books through interlibrary loan, encouraging me and checking facts. Without them none of it could have been done.

The many brides, grooms and clergy who gave unstintingly of their time likewise helped clarify my thoughts. Thank you all, especially Rev. Stephen Bergman, rector of St. Paul's Epsicopal Church in Medina, my unofficial PR agent, and Frank Stalf of the Lancaster Theological Seminary, Lancaster, Pennsylvania.

Last, my deepest appreciation goes to my editor, Rodney Clapp, who saw me through my first IVP venture and was with me all the way on this one too. Your friendship and encouragement mean everything.

1

Lifting the Veil on the "Storybook Wedding"

The bride-to-be's eyes swam with tears as she surveyed the slick spill of wedding information heaped in front of her on the kitchen table. Glossy magazines (some weighing a pound apiece), catalogs and vendors' brochures beckoned with designer gowns, heirloom bouquets and plastic videotape boxes slipcovered in "bridal" satin. Ever since her engagement was announced in the local newspaper three months ago, she had been been deluged with "fan mail" from everyone from cake bakers to videographers.

"All my life I've dreamed of planning my wedding," she said, giving the nearest pile a shove, "and now the time's finally here and it's like living in a nightmare. I wish I could just elope!"

Too many choices.

Not enough money.

Incessant arguments.

No time for anything but wedding, wedding, wedding.

A barrage of unsolicited advice.

The relentless quest for perfection.

Terror that something will go wrong and ruin the fantasy.

How did what began as a romantic proposal in the moonlight turn into a full-stage production complete with producer, choreographer, financial backers, balky actors, three stage managers, and a leading lady seriously considering the purchase of Sears best aluminum ladder?

"Every bride goes through this," her mother said, briskly dismissing it. "It's just wedding jitters. They're perfectly normal."

Normal? Well, at least the norm, anyway. If you haven't already learned it from personal experience—hold on to your veil. You're about to discover a nasty truth. There's something about wedding planning that brings out the worst in people—including you and the people you love most.

Formerly charming maids of honor throw fits over dresses they say make them look like an extra in Gone With The Wind. Dads refuse to walk brides down the aisle if their ex-wife's new husband is sitting in the pew. Moms thinks they're the one getting married and run the show like a five-star general. Grooms' families demand a German polka band when the bride's parents booked a string quartet. Brides don't want their soon-to-be sister-in-law in the wedding because she's pregnant and won't look right in the dress. Grooms decide the best course of action is to stay out of it, which makes everyone from the bride to her mother label him uninterested and uncooperative. And meanwhile all over town cash registers ring merrily as the medium-sized wedding agreed upon grows into a production worthy of Cecil B. DeMille.

A Shortfall of Roses

Everyone who has ever been involved in a wedding can trot out such horror stories. You probably know a few yourself and are determined not to star in one of your own. A wonderful, miraculous, holy thing has just happened in your life. You have found someone you love and who loves you back! Your heart sings with joy and awe because some-day soon this incredible person will stand at the altar of God and solemnly vow to forsake all others and cling only unto you—forever, all the days of your life. Sometimes it seems so dazzling you have to pinch yourself to make sure you're not dreaming.

But if you allow yourself to think seriously about it, it's actually a little scary too. Forever, by any standard, is a l-o-o-o-o-o-ong time. These days it could easily wind up being fifty years or more of life with the same person. That's a half-century's worth of laughter, tears, arguments, holidays, chores, bills, illnesses, in-laws and decisions, not to mention the peculiar complexities of retirement and old age. Working out a shared life of such duration takes time—time to be together sharing and negotiating, time with your pastor exploring issues, time for listening to the wisdom of those who have made the journey ahead of you, and time to be alone with your own prayers and reflections. Yet most couples, including those who place a high value on their spiritual lives, rarely allocate any more time toward planning their marriage than the church absolutely requires them to.

That's because planning the wedding gobbles practically every second. Hosting a fully orchestrated production for one hundred or more guests is a highly complex and complicated process. It costs the equivalent of three arms and four legs. You know little to nothing about what you are actually getting for your money. Your experience with entertaining on such a grand scale would fit into a nut cup with room to spare. Your expectations are through the roof. And everybody from your mother to your second cousin Jane in Dubuque knows exactly how you ought to do it and isn't shy about telling you.

Is it any wonder you forget that even the most extravagant wedding lasts only for a single day (okay, make that a couple of weeks, counting the showers, prewedding dinners and honeymoon), while a marriage is supposed to last a lifetime? The vast majority of couples spend a year or more, plus countless visits to florists, caterers, salons and photographers to plan two weeks of festivities and only around four visits to a clergyperson to plan a lifetime. And many by their own admission would even skip the four sessions if they could find a way to squirm out of them!

"Oh, we don't need to worry about that," one bride said confidently. "We've already talked about how many kids we want, sex, religion, in-laws, money, the works. We're perfectly compatible. The last thing we need is a minister to tell us what we already know."

Very likely you're echoing those very sentiments. You're not kids. You've dated a long while. You have an open, honest, trusting relationship. Great! But before you run off to your appointment with the caterer, think about something. The common belief is that one out of every two marriages ends in divorce. While that's enough to strike terror into the hearts of even the most ardent couple, professor Larry Bumpas of the University of Wisconsin says that if the 6.7 million separated Americans are added to the number of those who have already trekked to the courthouse for a divorce decree, the dissoultion rate actually stands at 60 percent! Of course you have no intention of joining the sad ranks. No one does. But the fact that you understand the solemnity of what you're about to do and would bet a Caribbean cruise on your compatibility doesn't mean you are immune to the stresses and stains of marriage new-millennium style.

You wouldn't dream of buying a house without actually seeing any houses or taking a job without exploring the salary, benefits and requirements. And yet houses can be sold and jobs changed with a lot less struggle, pain and spiritual angst than a covenant can be broken with God. Your engagement is a crucial time for doing the groundwork necessary for building a firm foundation. Never again will you have this much leisure and support to focus so intensely and completely on your relationship. But how on earth can you take advantage of it when planning the average American wedding leaves you feeling frazzled, pressured and brow-beaten? As you will soon see, the fault doesn't lie entirely with brides and grooms and misplaced priorities. It also lies with our culture which, when it comes to weddings, falls at least a dozen roses short of a bouquet.

The Wedding Machine
Almost as soon as the engagement ring slips into place, a huge white monster whirs into action. Gears grind, axles turn, and before you know it the two of you are on your way down the conveyor belt. By the time you reach the end you'll be stamped Bride and Groom, Made in America. The wedding business in this country is a 35 billion-dollar industry which claims a 91 percent market share of the average two million couples who exchange vows each year. Only 9 percent of all engaged couples choose a small, private ceremony. The rest opt for the traditional, formal wedding with as many of the trimmings as they can possibly swing.

Of course not all of them get caught up in the Wedding Machine. But sadly, many, if not most, do for the simple reason that the Machine is relentless and insidious and our culture has embraced it with open arms without paying so much as lip service to its high spiritual cost. Certainly, we mumble about the importance of marriage preparation classes and the high divorce rate. But once the church is booked for the third Saturday in October our focus immediately shifts to buffet versus sit-down dinner. Yet as important as it is to understand and truly believe that the wedding is less important than the marriage, that realization alone isn't enough. We also have to see that the high price tag dangling from the "typical" American wedding isn't just monetary. Only when we take a hard look at the stress, anguish and pettiness involved in the "typical" wedding will we begin to host smarter, saner, more gracious celebrations.

At this point you may be feeling a bit uncomfortable, as though the long white aisle runner were about to be pulled out from under your feet. Ever since you were old enough to mouth the words *ice sculptures,* you've been dreaming of the picture-perfect wedding. Why should you have to give that up just because you realize, maybe better than many brides and grooms, the gravity of what you are about to undertake? Is there no way to have a wonderful wedding without going financially, emotionally and spiritually bankrupt?

First off, this isn't the antiwedding book. Its purpose is not to convince you that wanting a traditional wedding is tantamount to moral collapse. Hosting a wedding together can be a creative, joyful event, not to mention a great learning experience. If you approach it in the spirit of love and true hospitality it can actually enhance the work you're doing together and with your pastor. Planning a wedding together can help you explore your values, set priorities, learn the art of compromise, work in tandem for a common purpose, and deal with real-life money issues. It can also help set a positive tone for your future relationship with both sides of the family, as well as deepen the bonds between you and your future spouse.

So go ahead—have a wedding! Only don't go shopping just yet. There is plenty of time to pick out your colors, silver pattern and reception menu. First it's essential to understand the power of the Wedding Machine, how it got that power and the damage it can do to your life and your spirit if you let it control you.

Victoria's (Wedding) Secrets

Extravagant weddings are nothing new, of course. Even in biblical times people celebrated marriages with the equivalent of a gala reception, as evidenced by the wedding feast of Cana where Mary implored Jesus to change water into wine when the refreshments ran out early. In almost all cultures and all ages a wedding has traditionally been a time to throw caution to the wind. Many of those very early celebrations, in fact, spawned the traditions we still cherish today, such as tossing the bridal bouquet, exchanging rings and placing a "lucky" coin in the bride's shoe.

But the event that set the standard for what we recognize as today's traditional "storybook wedding" is the marriage of Queen Victoria and Prince Albert in 1840. When it comes to excess, this pair wrote the book. The queen's gown alone cost a thousand pounds sterling and required one hundred lace makers to work for six months straight. When it was finished, the lace patterns were destroyed so no one else could copy the dress (as if anyone else could afford it!). At a time when the line of demarcation between poverty and middle-class comfort was ten shillings, or a half pound a week, it would have taken the average family thirty-eight and a half years of full wages to pay it off! Getting the queen and her sumptuous gown (which some historians have called "a tasteless muddle") down the aisle of the Chapel Royal at St. James was no easy task either—it required the services of a dozen white-clad train-bearers and a cadre of trumpeters. On the day of the wedding ferocious winds blew and sheets of rain pelted the city, but all of London thronged the streets to see the spectacle.

While you probably have no plans for a custom-designed dress by top bridal designer Vera Wang or vocals by the Mormon Tabernacle Choir, you most likely do have a very clear idea of what a wedding should be. If so, you aren't alone. Throughout the twentieth century brides have craved cathedral-length trains, veils with tiaras and sit-down dinners for three hundred of their closest friends and family. Only during the Depression, World War 2 and the protest years of the late 1960s and early 1970s did the demand for wedding finery take a nose-dive—and during two of those periods it wasn't even by choice. Worldwide financial meltdown made extravagant weddings nearly impossible during the Depression, while patriotism far superseded personal interests for the duration of World War II. The June 1943 issue of *Harper's* magazine probably summed up the intense flag-waving of the 1940s best when it declared, "Shower no rice on this year's honeymooners. You can't waste good starch on sentiment!" With a nation in crisis and almost every American family worried about a loved one overseas, fripperies such as lily of the valley flown in from the south of France and five-piece live bands seemed embarrassingly self-indulgent, if not nearly impossible to procure.

That means that the only ones who deliberately gave the wedding industry the cold shoulder were the hippie brides and grooms of the Vietnam era—the very same people who today are forking over big bucks so their sons and daughters can traipse down the aisle in style. No embroidered Mexican cotton, daisy wreaths and bare feet for the offspring of the Woodstock Generation. The traditional Wedding Machine has never been so well oiled as it is at this moment. During the Reagan years when the gross national product was strong and most consumers had money in their pockets, the wedding industry bloomed like a hothouse orchid. Ever since, new products and services—one-of-a-kind wedding invitations made from handmade paper, live Monarch butterflies shipped in the larva stage for release when the couple leaves the church, wedding insurance and videographers who will not only film the big day but dice, splice and set it to music—are tripping over each other to flood an already flooded market.

The wedding industry came of age by realizing one essential thing—consumers will pay staggering sums for anything with the word *wedding* or *bridal* printed on the label. One bride told of going to a fabric store to buy tulle in which to wrap Jordan almonds as favors for her guests. The clerk directed her to a bolt of white fabric marked "bridal tulle." Fortunately just as she prepared to purchase several yards, her friend spotted another bolt of tulle in a different part of the store. It was white. It was exactly the same weight as the "bridal" variety. But it was priced at only a third of the cost!

Another bride whose dress was exactly the same style and fabric as her attendants' dresses reported a huge price discrepancy when after the wedding she and her friends took their wedding finery to be dry cleaned. The bridesmaids' dresses were listed on the invoice as "prom dresses" and priced at fifteen dollars apiece, while the white dress was deemed a "wedding gown" and as such charged thirty dollars—exactly twice as much!

Outrageous? Of course. But to put the entire onus of blame on the shoulders of wedding vendors isn't quite playing fair when consumers snap up lace-trimmed sneakers at fifty dollars a pop so the bride can be comfortable at the reception. According to the wedding industry, today's brides and grooms actively regale manufacturers, retailers and service providers with requests for ever more dazzling, exotic and expensive choices. The Wedding Machine is fueled by a consumer mentality which believes deeply and passionately that a wedding must be perfect down to the last grain of rice. That's why we rush to newsstands in droves for the gorgeous, glossy bridal books which, as you probably already know, are comprised mostly of ads for pricey, drop-dead diamonds, gowns, cakes, flowers, honeymoons and home decor. In 1997 *Bride's*, the leader of the pack, ran 3,015 pages of advertising, while *Modern Bride* ran 2,640.

What's interesting about all this is the fact that we are paying more serious homage to the traditional wedding than ever before at a time when the divorce rate is the highest in history, record numbers of couples are living together before tying the knot and the standard for the "ideal" marriage is more egalitarian than it has ever been. On the surface it doesn't seem to make much sense. If both economic and social factors are giving marriage an overhaul, at least in the secular world, why ever would we cling so tenaciously to the classic image of the blushing bride and her phalanx of attendants?

The answer may well lie in cultural myth. More than one young woman whose marriage wound up in the courtroom has gone on *Oprah* to publicly admit that what drove her down the aisle was the intense desire to experience the glamour of the white wedding. Not love. Not companionship. Not shared goals. Not religious beliefs. Not even the ticking of the biological clock. But the overwhelming need to be The Bride.

The Princess Bride

From the time little girls are old enough to play with Wedding Barbie and dress up as brides for Halloween with lace curtains on their heads and bouquets of plastic flowers clutched in their hot little hands, they are spoon-fed the myth of the Princess Bride. Either directly or by inference, the message is clear—to be a bride is to experience the happiest, most extraordinary day of your life. If you haven't already done so, you will soon find out that wedding vendors can hardly contain their glee. They may not have planted this notion in the heads of American women, but they are certainly not about to do anything to dispel it either.

"What's another hundred dollars?" they say, urging you to indulge every whim. "After all, it *is* the most important day of your life."

Well, when you put it like *that* . . .

What's so great about this line of reasoning is that it pushes parental guilt buttons just as effectively as it tempts brides to overspend.

"This is the happiest day of your daughter's life," vendors purr as they present your mother with a twinkly smile and a bill the size of the national debt. "She's only a bride once, you know."

Never mind that the latter isn't even true for more than half of all brides. The point is, it sells merchandise by keeping alive the comforting belief that this marriage is different from all the rest—a keeper in a world of throwbacks. Of course given your sense of commitment and your understanding of the responsibilities of marriage, there's a good chance that your marriage actually will be one of the ones which survive and flourish. But even so, are you really ready to concede that at age twenty-three or twenty-six or thirty you will never again experience the same height of sublime joy as you experience on your wedding day? Does God dole out only one glorious moment per customer?

Besides being ludicrous the cultural icon of the princess bride is dangerous. Besides compromising your ability to see clearly whether or not you are making the right choice in a mate, it greedily snatches precious time and attention away from your marriage and fosters a sense of entitlement that eats away at your soul. No matter what the state of your and/or your parents' finances, it assures you that you deserve a lavish wedding. So what if you wind up acting self-indulgent, regal and—okay, admit it—a little greedy? Such behavior is perfectly okay, it promises you. After all, a big white wedding is every woman's birthright! If others fight for the spotlight or refuse to help you make every dream come true, then *they* are clearly the ones failing *you*.

Of course most brides don't begin planning their weddings with this thought uppermost in their minds. But as the drama unfolds and obstacles pop up in the way of the fantasy, it slowly and insidiously worms its way aboveground. Also, as more and more grooms take an active role in planning and helping to pay for the wedding, they too can begin feeling as if they deserve only the very best and friends and family have an unspoken obligation to see to it that they get it.

According to industry analysts, the cost of today's "average" American wedding rings in to the tune of sixteen thousand dollars, with the figure rising dramatically in big cities such as New York, Boston and Los Angeles. For most families such a sizable nest egg equals two years' tuition (plus room and board) at a state university, a brand-new midsize car or the down payment on a house. To allow such a sum to ride on a single day of romantic fantasy would seem unthinkable. Yet it is not unthinkable. The formal wedding is seen by our society almost as a rite of passage, like orthodontia, summer camp and a college diploma.

With this acceptance of the lavish wedding as an agreeable and even necessary expense, and with so much money at stake for a single day, it's no wonder anxiety, stress and fear override love, tolerance and even common sense. Everybody wants a say in how the money is to be spent because everybody wants to make sure that the return is worth the high cost. But what exactly is this return anyway? And is it the same for everyone? Here is where it gets a little dicey.

Most parents, as well as most engaged couples, would be quick to reply that the return is a day of unparalleled happiness, a joyous gathering of the clans to celebrate one of life's most important milestones. And certainly that's a big component. But to say that it is the sole expectation is both naive and dishonest. Weddings stir up deep feelings about status and self-worth, not only in the marrying couple but in their parents as well. Consciously or subconsciously, you can't help but wonder what your choices, your budget, your guest list and even the gifts you request and receive are saying to the community about who you are. The Wedding Machine understands and feeds this—very often fifty-dollar-a-plate dinners of stuffed chicken royale you can't afford.

A Simply Beautiful Antidote

Fortunately, it doesn't have to be this way. You can create a lovely, romantic, unforgettable day by simply changing your mind! Instead of viewing your wedding as a sort of elaborate set piece in which you are the star, try thinking about it as an opportunity to be true to yourself and your core beliefs. Throughout the New Testament Jesus asks us repeatedly to do that which is at once the most simple and difficult thing on earth—to love one another. Wholly. Completely. Without judgment. Imagine the outcome if you were to keep that in mind when

☐ your mother wants to invite the cousins from Pittsburgh you can't stand

☐ the estimate from the florist comes in at twice what you can afford

☐ the groom announces he wants powder-blue tuxedos

☐ your best friend is fifty pounds overweight and you have your heart set on the bridesmaids wearing red column dresses

☐ the church says no to secular music, including both "your" song and the theme song from *Aladdin*

☐ the romantic inn you want to book for your reception isn't handicap accessible and your grandmother can't negotiate the spiral staircase

By rethinking what a wedding is, exploring what you really want and allowing your choices to reflect the pure love of God, you can have a *simply* beautiful wedding that will be everything you dreamed of and more. All that will be missing are the family feuds, hurt feelings, staggering bills, overdrawn accounts and paralyzing anxiety that make so many couples miserable. Later in this book you will be invited to share the special wedding day of a real-life couple who put the simply beautiful principles to work with stunning results. You will also be given the opportunity to reflect on how each component of the typical wedding contributes to its overall effect, as well as some points to think about as you make your own choices. But first let's define *simply* so you can rid your mind of the image of a generic wedding packaged in a dull black-and-white box!

If you have already dipped into the luscious pages of the bridal magazines, you are very likely suspicious of the word *simply*. You have your sights set on a Carolina Herreras gown that made you catch your breath the first time you saw it. Naturally you aren't too eager to sign on for anything that suggests you can't or shouldn't have it. To you *simply* conjures up a no-frills day that begins with a series of blue-light specials and winds up with punch and cake in the church basement—hardly the stuff of which dreams are made.

Plain, unadorned and—uh—cheap is certainly one way of looking at the word *simply*. But let's throw out that definition and consider another. *Simply* also connotes purity of form, easy elegance and natural grace. Of course what you describe as "simply beautiful" may be something totally different from what your best friend, your sister or the woman at the next desk in your office chooses. And that is the best part of all—*simply* beautiful means that you have total freedom to be yourself without worrying what others might think.

The simply beautiful wedding is not a set-in-concrete dictum but rather a state of mind, heart and spirit. Whether your particular spin on it includes a designer gown and a stretch limo is up to you. Which frills you ultimately wind up with matter far less than how comfortably you can afford them, why you feel you need to have them, how you go about getting them and how authentically you extend your hospitality to those who come to share your joy. The most important feature of every simply beautiful wedding is the fact that it is totally love-centered. Anything that causes undue stress, pain or feelings that fail to reflect the love of God is eliminated. Period. Otherwise you have total freedom to plan the kind of wedding that will set the tone for a simply beautiful life.

There's a lovely old Shaker hymn that speaks a deep and abiding truth: "And when we find ourselves in the place just right, 'twill be in the valley of love and delight." Find the "place just right" for you and you will need to impress no one. They will already be impressed—by the miracle of your love and the wisdom of your heart.

2

Till Debt
Do Us Part

My parents are acting like we're kids," *Laura complained,* her dark eyes snapping with indignation. "They need to back off and let us make our own decisions!"

Laura and her fiancé, Larry, plan to be married next spring. They are both twenty-six, just out of graduate school and beginning career-level jobs, Laura as a high-school art teacher and Larry in advertising. Long before he slipped a one-carat diamond engagement ring on her finger less than two weeks ago, they knew that within three years of their marriage they want to buy a house, have a baby and begin a home-based design business. They also knew that a major goal was to free up their weekends in order to take on the responsibility of running their church youth group, a ministry that badly needs their youth, energy and commitment.

But—here's the rub—they also have their hearts set on a big wedding. Laura envisions stargazer lilies—*lots* of stargazer lilies—and a horse-drawn carriage to carry them away from the church in style. Larry is talking tuxedos with tails and romantic ten-day cruises.

"We've been together practically since the beginning of college," he said, a touch defensively. "That's almost seven years. We deserve a big wedding just for our astounding longevity!"

"We're really not materialistic people," Laura added. "For both of us family comes first. But this is something that means a lot to us. My parents don't have a clue why it's so important."

Not long ago Laura's father tried to suggest that planning a twenty-thousand-dollar wedding doesn't make a whole lot of sense when you don't actually *have* twenty thousand dollars. He reminded Laura and Larry of their goals and suggested that if they continue opting for an extravaganza they may have to put those aims on the back burner. Nonetheless, in less than two weeks' time they have managed to

☐ place a one-thousand-dollar deposit on a reception for 350 guests in the ballroom of a stately historic mansion

☐ begin moonlighting on weekends, Laura cashiering at a discount store, Larry delivering pizzas

☐ write a "subtle" letter to Laura's grandmother in Florida announcing their engagement in hopes of garnering a contribution to the wedding fund

☐ wheedle six thousand dollars out of Laura's parents, who still have a son in college, and an additional one thousand out of Larry's mother, a widow who works for minimum wage

☐ amass an impressive collection of slick travel brochures for cruises in the Gulf of Mexico

At first glance you might be tempted to say, "So what? They're young—they'll buy the house, start the business and have the baby later"—all of which is quite true. They certainly have plenty of time to do all of those things and more. But probe a little deeper and see if you don't touch a sensitive nerve.

Ouch! Thought so.

All of these seemingly harmless wedding plans are clouding some very serious spiritual issues, including financial stewardship, long-term goals, the use of time and even what it is morally right to expect from your parents and relatives. But like so many well-intentioned couples Laura and Larry have never given a thought to the spiritual implications of their choices.

It's not that they are essentially superficial, mercenary or self-absorbed people. Laura was right when she said they normally give rampant competitive consumerism a wide berth. But they are crazy in love, excited about the future and so caught up in the thrill of their new status as an engaged couple that they haven't stopped to think clearly. They know full well that they are about to embark upon a serious, lifelong commitment, but in a way it is that very understanding which makes them feel driven to do everything on a grand scale. With only one shot at it, they figure they have to get it "right."

You may be feeling much the same way. Getting married is fun and exciting. You're suddenly the center of so much attention and so many questions. Are you having a sit-down dinner or a buffet? How many bridesmaids will there be? Have you decided where to go on your honeymoon? Decisions and possibilities whirl through your mind like painted ponies on a brightly lit carousel. But lose sight of the brass ring for even a single moment and you could wind up seriously compromising the very things you want most—a home, a family and the peace of mind that comes from being true to your core beliefs and goals.

After they pay for their rings, wedding and honeymoon, Laura and Larry will have spent slightly less than half of their combined income for a year, including the money they will have made moonlighting. After such a major outlay of cash, there is no way they can begin to think seriously about buying a home, having a baby or beginning a business. Although they say they expect to pay cash for almost everything they buy for the wedding, it will still take them at least five years to recoup what they have spent—which in essence means that they will be "paying" for their wedding and honeymoon for half a decade!

Substance Abuse

The prophet Isaiah asks, "Why do you spend your money for that which is not bread and your labor for that which does not satisfy?" (Isaiah 55:2). Down through the ages the question echoes—ancient, urgent and wise. Consider it carefully before you get entangled in one of the many moving parts of the Wedding Machine. Do you really want to spend all that you have and much of what you don't yet have on things of no substance?

Before you answer, be sure to think hard about the concept of substance. At first glance it would seem to apply only to nondurable goods, or cheap gimmicky junk, which of course you have no intention of buying for your wedding. But even the handmade, museum-quality, moiré guestbook with the exquisite satin roses has no substance for *you* if in order to buy it you sacrifice something of far greater value. Beautiful objects do indeed delight the eye and feed the soul, but the question you must ask yourself is, will they still warm your heart twenty-five years from now? How about next year when the wedding and the honeymoon are over and the Princess Bride has vanished into the ether, leaving in her place a woman who yearns to hold her first child and close the door of her own house when the day is done? Perhaps the guestbook from the card shop at the mall is pretty enough after all. Though most brides cherish wedding memories, all agree that once the party is over and they return from their honeymoon to "join the real world," the importance of moiré guestbooks fades faster than the dye in the bridesmaids' shoes.

A survey conducted by *Bride's* magazine reported that a full 73 percent of all engaged couples say they expect money to be a major problem in their married life. Yet that belief doesn't stop them from going so far as to take out loans to pay for their weddings. Since couples are older when they marry these days—in 1990 the median age for first-time brides was 23.9 and 26.3 for grooms—many pay for all or most of their weddings themselves. Even when parents agree to pay the lion's share, many couples chip in for the simple reason that their wants outstrip their parents' ability to pay. Despite climbing housing costs, car payments on their first new vehicles and, very often, college loan debt, they willingly walk out on a shaky financial limb to breathe life into fantasies that have no more substance than gossamer clouds.

According to a national study by Nellie Mae, the country's largest nonprofit provider of college loans, the average new college graduate's debt has more than doubled in the past six years due to higher tuition and a shift in aid from grants, which don't have to be paid back, to loans which do. With the average college loan hovering at eighteen thousand dollars, some couples find it necessary to delay marriage altogether.

Even if you are one of the lucky ones who aren't going to begin married life with huge built-in debt, think through your short-term goals before you set a budget for your simply beautiful wedding. It's impossible to decide how much you want to spend until you figure out how much you realistically *can* spend without jeopardizing your goals and values. Remember, this is your first major joint decision as a couple. How well you make it—and honor it—can set the tone for your future financial transactions. Remember, too, that the very retailers who are enticing you with wedding finery and household goods understand this very well. They know that if they can kindle a spark of acquisitiveness right now, at this vulnerable juncture in your lives, there is a very good chance it will burst into the eternal flame and keep you spending and spending and spending . . .

Emotion in Motion

But as crucial as logic and determination are in making wise fiscal choices, you also need to bear in mind the fact that the path to the altar is littered with as many good intentions as rose petals. Countless couples start out with a realistic vision only to trip over the biggest stumbling block of all—sentiment. If cultural myth and consumerism drive the Wedding Machine, then sentiment sits in the passenger seat playing Motown on the radio and reading the road map! With one thumb firmly on the nostalgic past and the other on the shining future, it knows exactly how to manipulate your emotions. Faster than you can say "freesia" nostalgia and idealism can kick into high gear, leaving you feeling as though your wedding must conform to a set of standards based more on sentiment than on reason.

One young bride told the story of going with her mother and future mother-in-law to try on wedding gowns. She had done her homework, knew the price of a moderate gown and was determined to stick to it. But when she got to the salon, she immediately spotted a dress reminiscent of the one her grandmother had worn in 1949—same sweetheart neckline, same heavy satin, same cathedral train—and knew she "had to have it," even though it cost three times what she had planned to spend.

"It's like my brain shut off," she admitted a year later. "All of a sudden it was the most important thing in the world. Even my mom got into it. Gram's gown had been lost in a fire, and we thought she'd get a kick out of me getting one almost just like it. All we could talk about was how great the two portraits of us would look hanging side by side on the wall."

In retrospect she wishes she had not ordered any dress at all that day.

"When you're feeling frantic to have something, that's when you shouldn't spend a penny," she said with a wry grin. "We should have gone home and thought it over. I'll bet anything we would have either bought a less expensive dress with some of the same features somewhere else or maybe looked into having one made. I know we wouldn't have spent that kind of money. How much we love Gram had absolutely nothing to do with me having that particular gown, gorgeous though it was. We just went temporarily crazy! If only I could have that money back, I could get decent living-room furniture . . ."

As you can see, couples aren't the only ones whose emotions are at risk when it comes to wedding shopping. Parents too fall prey to the nostalgia trap, particularly when they see that their children have their hearts set on something. Perhaps they had a huge wedding themselves and want to give their daughter the same experience. Or more likely they didn't have all the bells and whistles at their own weddings and are determined to make up for what they lacked by giving it to their child. Either way, when faced with a daughter whose face is shining like a newly minted silver dollar, it's difficult for moms and dads to say no, especially when sentiment whispers such heart-tugging lines as

☐ "She'll never be your little girl again."

☐ "It seems like only yesterday . . ."

☐ "She's dreamed of this all her life. How can you disappoint her?"

If parents have the money to indulge their children's wedding fantasies and choose of their own volition to do so, that's one thing, but the fact is that many do not have the deep pockets you may believe they have. Weddings tend to crop up at a most inopportune time in parents' lives—the juncture between their children's college education and their own retirement. This is when most middle-aged couples realize that if they hope to ensure a secure future for themselves they need to play catch-up. For many years their children's needs took every spare penny. Now finally they are at a point where it may be possible to make up for lost time, and then—wham—wedding debt looms on the horizon like the four horsemen of the apocalypse.

Before you even sit down to talk with your parents about the possibility of a contribution to your wedding fund, consider their long-term needs. Not only will it keep you from requesting more than they can comfortably give, but it will also help you put a check on sentiment before they unwittingly get swept away in a tide of tender feelings for you. Putting someone else's needs ahead of your own wants is never easy to do, and it is especially difficult when you stand on the brink of such an exciting adventure. Bridal shows, books and magazines bombard you with tantalizing images, your engaged friends rhapsodize over fondant-draped cakes with three-dimensional sugar pansies and raspberry filling, and here you are being asked to make a tough decision.

But if you make the choice to act with love, you will reap dividends that will continue long after the party is over and the last slice of (expensive) cake is gone. Choosing love over even the most deeply cherished fantasies demonstrates a maturity that will serve you well in the years to come when you are asked again and again to put your spouse or your children first. It also gives you an opportunity to give your parents a priceless gift and sets the tone for a more relaxed and loving engagement and wedding.

Those Wicked Little Wants

But letting your parents off the financial hook is only half the battle. There still comes a point where you have to grapple with how much money you think you need. The fact that you recognize that Mom and Dad can't afford to book the country club for a Saturday night in June doesn't automatically mean you have a complete handle on the money issue. The "wants" have a nasty way of cropping up in other ways and making you feel as though it is perfectly okay to do things you wouldn't normally dream of doing. This doesn't just mean taking out loans, or moonlighting, or selling your piano to raise cash—it means literally going begging.

Laura and Larry brushed up against this when they decided to write the "engagement announcement" letter to Laura's grandmother in Florida. Though they were by no means overt about asking for a handout, they both knew deep down that the purpose of the letter was more monetary than celebratory. In order to justify sending it they assured themselves that Grandma had plenty of money and would actually welcome the opportunity to write them a hefty check. Perhaps they were even right about that. Wealthy grandparents very often do want to share the goodies and pamper their grandchildren a bit. But is it fair to expect them to? Is it a loving act to view them as a vehicle that can be ever so subtly manipulated for profit?

Laura and Larry's letter may seem rather minor compared to what some couples have resorted to, and in a way it is. But where do you draw the line? How different are they really in spirit from the couple who unwittingly wound up in syndicated adviser Ann Landers's column not long ago? A woman wrote to Ann saying that she had received a mass mailing from friends flat-out asking for a donation to help cover wedding costs. It arrived complete with a return envelope and a section to detach and send back showing the amount of the donation. The recipient was so appalled she wasn't sure how to respond.

"The expenses involved are overwhelming and we humbly request your help," the letter writers implored. "We ask that each of you dig into your hearts and graciously assist us with whatever financial contribution you can make."

Dig into your hearts? We won't even go there—it's not a pretty image. But aesthetics aside, the request clearly sugarcoats a deep-rooted sense of entitlement with such upstanding words as *humbly* and *graciously*. You can wrap it up in silver foil and trim it with satin bows, but the fact is, if it looks like a duck and quacks like a duck, underneath all the glitter it's still a duck.

Obviously the letter writers felt entitled to something they couldn't have and felt justified to take measures that very likely ran amok of their own value system. Of course you wouldn't resort to anything so tacky yourself, but whether or not you would actually send such a letter may be less important than the feelings that generated it. As long as you share those feelings and allow them to rule you, your wedding plans are guaranteed to be fraught with anger, anxiety and ungratefulness.

Play the Flip Side

"But what I can I do about it?" one bride asked. "I can't help the way I feel, can I?"

You may not be able to keep the feelings from cropping up, but you can certainly choose to change them when they do. Happiness is always a choice. It doesn't fly around like the proverbial bluebird, swooping willy-nilly past one person and landing gracefully on the shoulder of another. You have to choose it, especially when things are not exactly to your liking.

For at least a decade social scientists have conducted studies aimed at predicting how much money people need to be happy. The surprising upshot is that more money does not equal more happiness. What researchers found is that we need enough money to meet our basic survival needs with a little extra left over for pleasure. Once that ideal is reached, our happiness quotient does not rise regardless of how much our net worth does. Certainly more money can give you a temporary high, but scientists have discovered that the euphoria lasts for no more than about three weeks at best. Only when you are starving, freezing or in dire need of something crucial such as medical care will the sudden acquisition of more money contribute to your overall sense of well-being over the long run. Happiness, the studies point out, is much more strongly tied to family life, interpersonal relationships and work than it is to money.

So even if you won one of the numerous contests that offer a free wedding as the grand prize, there is no guarantee you would be any happier than you are with the budget you have now. For one thing, the more money you spend, the higher your anxiety rises. What if it a storm blows up, topples the white tent and sends masses of freesia and roses flying through the air like litter in a fast-food restaurant parking lot? What if the middle tier of the hand-painted cake gives way while you are cutting it? What if the flower girl spills Coke all over her designer dress five minutes before the organ begins to play "The Wedding March"? The more money there is at stake, the harder it is to laugh at wedding disasters—and the harder it is to relax and allow the day to unfold.

As one wedding consultant put it, "I never saw a moderate wedding turn into a disaster. Sure wish I could say that about some of the high-end ones."

More money can also create problems you might never have even considered. One couple shared just such an unhappy experience. While shopping for a reception hall they discovered a wonderful facility that had two rooms—a large one that accommodated up to 250 people and a smaller one that comfortably held 130. Since they expected to invite only 125 guests, the second room seemed made to order—except for one catch. The larger room offered a breathtaking lake vista and the smaller faced the road. In order to book the room with the view they had to guarantee payment for 175 meals—50 more than would ever be eaten even if everyone showed up. No way could they consider it. But not long after they reluctantly placed a deposit on the roadside space, the groom's uncle agreed to make up the difference for the large room as his gift to the couple. They were elated.

"Until the wedding, that is," the bride said ruefully. "It was a disaster. We had one hundred guests actually attend, and they were swallowed up in such an enormous space. There was no sense of intimacy at all. Hardly anybody danced, and by ten o'clock the party was pretty much over."

A second point to consider is that despite what a consumer society would have you believe, the Beatles had it right back in the sixties when they sang "Money can't buy me love." As researcher Michael Argyle points out, "The happiness people derive from consumption is based on whether they consume more than their neighbors, or more than they did in the past." Richard A. Easterlin, an economist at the University of Southern California, concurs. Money can buy happiness, he concludes, but only if the amounts keep getting bigger and other people aren't getting more. The bottom line is, we feel well off if we have more than our peers and poor if we have less.

Consumerism also leads you to begin to viewing people as commodities, much as Laura and Larry did when they wrote the letter to her grandmother, and lessens your appreciation of what you do have. How can you truly experience the special joy of your engagement or take deep delight in the surprise shower your sorority sisters throw when you are obsessed with the fact that you can't afford to hire a live band? What's more, a bad case of consumeritis can make you feel as if you have to outshine every wedding you've ever been to—when the truth is that no matter how unique or spectacular your taste, ideas and budget, there is always going to be someone who does it bigger.

After watching a TV program about movie stars' weddings, one young bride felt driven to decorate the back of every dinner guest's chair with a cascade of fresh flowers and ribbons.

"It cost a fortune. A *for*tune!" she groaned. "I couldn't really afford it, but I did it anyway. And then no sooner did the credit card bill come in than I went to a friend's wedding and she did the same thing using inexpensive baskets and flowers from her aunt's garden. It cost her like an eighth of what I paid—and am still paying for—and hers looked every bit as good as mine had, or at least good enough!"

The key to feeling satisfied with the situation in which you find yourself is to take the word *ungrateful,* flip it over—and find gratitude. Begin with a prayer of thanksgiving for the miracle and blessing of love. Then follow with one for the gift of creativity—something all of us have but few fully use.

Couples who tap into their creativity very often get what they want (or a reasonable facsimile) without breaking the bank. The idea is not to find ways to take advantage of anyone, but rather to use your own ingenuity to create something wonderful. One of the most creative weddings stories is told by a young couple from Massachusetts who pulled off an unusual and beautiful celebration with a minuscule budget—slightly more than one-tenth of the national average. With so little cash to work with it would seem impossible to reach their twin goals—elegance and an abundance of friends and family—but they did it by breaking their wedding day into components rather than seeing it as a unified whole.

As a brilliant gold sun rose over the ocean at Cape Cod on a perfect May morning, the bride and groom, along with their parents, siblings and two closest friends, joined the minister for an exquisite, intimate, deeply moving ceremony on the beach. The bride looked radiant in a full-length beaded gown with a sweep train and full-length veil, all purchased at a deep discount from the close-out rack at the fanciest bridal salon in the city. Following the service, the small group convened at a lovely old inn for an elegant-down-to-the-last-crystal-goblet breakfast. Later that evening they changed into casual clothes and welcomed a huge crowd of well-wishers for a clambake on the same beach where they had been married. Not only did the bills come in right at budget, but a year later people are still talking about what a great party it was.

It's like the parable of the talents in the Bible. Abundance didn't come to the man who took the one talent, buried it in the ground and upon his master's return presented it to him intact and totally unchanged. Rather, it came to the two who took what they were given and multiplied it. By using the talents with which God has already provided you, you can create abundance in both your wedding and your life—whether you begin with five "talents," two or only one.

A Case of Galloping Consumption

Of course there's abundance and there's also a miserable disease known as galloping consumption. In days gone by "galloping consumption" was the term used to refer to tuberculosis. Here on the brink of the twenty-first century it has taken on a whole new meaning. Galloping consumption is what hits you when you're out wedding shopping and your credit card starts sending up smoke signals. Even if funds are tight, you can come down with a case serious enough to require intervention. But if you find yourself among the tiny minority of couples for whom money is not a problem, you may be especially vulnerable. Wash your hands, hold your breath, and don't talk to anyone whose title begins with a *c*—especially calligraphers, consultants and caterers—until you've had a chance to take stock.

Popular columnist Dave Barry once quipped, "Your wedding is sacred—it should cost a lot!" Like any good humorist Barry homed right in on the absurdity of the thing. It doesn't take a theologian to tell you that conspicuous consumption is the very antithesis of Judeo-Christian values at any time, but most especially so when you are preparing for a passage as deeply spiritual as marriage. We've already established that to clothe yourself in humility as the Bible repeatedly exhorts us all to do doesn't mean that you have to drag down the aisle in sackcloth and ashes. (You get to wear the Carolina Herreras, remember?) But it does suggest the need to carefully consider the point at which your dreams slip out of the realm of rare indulgence and enter the dangerous ground of excess. Excess is the point where the emphasis shifts from grateful celebration to self-glorification.

You will know you are there when

☐ you begin ordering people around like a bureaucrat drunk on power

☐ you find yourself dropping names of brands, stores, pricey service providers and even potential guests

☐ you complain about things of which you are actually quite proud, as in "My caterer is driving me crazy! She must call me a million times a day about hors d'oeuvres. Do I want black caviar or red? What does she think I hired her for anyway?"

☐ the wedding has taken over your life to the point where even the time you spend with your fiancé is consumed by it

☐ you are embarrassed to admit how much you actually spent, and/or you are collaborating with your mother to keep the full extent of the bills from your father's knowledge until after the wedding

☐ you expect rules to be bent to accommodate your every whim

☐ you are actively seeking to outdo someone or "make a splash"

☐ you keep looking at dresses, rings, flowers and so on after you have made your selections and ordered them

☐ you are never satisfied with the merchandise and services available to you, and when you do finally reach a decision, you repeatedly find fault with the finished product, even when you have gone to great lengths to acquire it

If you recognize yourself in any, or too many, of the above examples, it may be wise to slow down and rethink what it is you want your wedding to reflect. One couple, Amy and Chuck, who were in their early thirties when they married and both quite successful in their fields, found themselves in the midst of planning a reception so lavish Amy now calls it "obscene."

"The W-word is armed and dangerous," she says. "We say 'wedding' and all of a sudden we're on a spendathon. Whether you have a lot of money or a little money isn't really the point. The point is, a wedding is a religious rite followed by a party. A party. Not the coronation of the queen of England."

Amy's wake-up call came when she and her younger sister went shopping for crystal bowls in which to float gardenias and candles on each table at the reception. At a local department store they found exactly what they wanted and Amy wasted no time asking the clerk to write up an order for thirty bowls at thirty dollars apiece. The bill didn't faze her until her sister suddenly said, "What are you going to do with thirty crystal bowls after the wedding? It's not like anybody really needs that many."

Amy says the offhand remark froze her in midtransaction. To her amazement, she felt ashamed. Of course she wouldn't use them again. They would probably sit wrapped up in boxes in the basement for years, or else she would end up giving them as wedding gifts to everybody she knew. Immediately she told the clerk she wanted to think about it some more, walked away—and didn't go back. Instead she took the money she would have spent and asked her minister to use it at his discretion to make someone else's wedding dreams come true.

"I don't want to sound like your mother saying, 'Think of all those starving children in India,' " she says, laughing, "but the point is, Chuck and I were able to spread the wealth, pull off one exceedingly fine wedding and feel good knowing that our happiness would touch others in a tangible way."

Money, be it a little or a lot, requires responsibility. Before you spend it on your wedding, ask yourself three questions.

☐ Does this purchase have real, lasting value?

☐ Why am I buying it?

☐ Does it give glory to God?

Listen carefully to the answers and let them lead you where they inevitably will—down the aisle to a simply beautiful wedding.

3

Tradition or Tyranny?

The *young bride-to-be frowned as the reception hall manager* described the elaborate silver swags she would use to decorate the table where the bridal party would sit during the reception. "But I don't want any of that," the younger woman finally ventured. "I just want us all to mingle with the guests. No bridal table."

"No bridal table!" the manager yelped in disbelief. Had she been able to faint and still express the full depth of her disapproval, she'd have been splayed across the elegant black-and-white tile floor like a bearskin rug. "But everybody has a head table! It's *traditional.*"

Ah yes, the T-word. Sooner or later it works its way into practically every decision you make for your wedding. Expect to hear it often because when it comes to pulling your pursestrings it's almost as effective as the W-word—which may very well explain why the two are so often uttered in the same breath! Tradition can fill your wedding day with deep meaning and lovely memories, but it can also make you more miserable than you ever imagined. That's why right from the start it's important to understand that the fact that a secular custom is "traditional" doesn't mean you are required by God or the bridal police to have it at your wedding. Very often the word *traditional* gets bandied about when something is (a) expensive, (b) complicated, (c) uncomfortable or (d) all of the above!

The cathedral-length train, the veil and the tuxedo are all "traditional" wedding accouterments, as are the tiered cake, the lengthy honeymoon, the bevy of bridesmaids and the formal portrait. It's traditional to toss the bouquet, throw the garter, feed each other wedding cake and clink glasses at the reception so the bride and groom will kiss. Engraved invitations with tissue inserts, reception cards and wedding favors likewise reek of tradition, as do the rehearsal dinner, the bridesmaids' shower and "The Wedding March." But whoever said that any wedding worth its orange blossoms has to have all this stuff anyway?

As you may recall, Queen Victoria got the ball rolling with her wedding to Prince Albert. Elaborate though this event was, however, it proved to be merely a dress rehearsal for the extravanganza she hosted for her daughter in 1858. The day Victoria Adelaide Mary, the Princess Royal, joined Prince Frederick William of Prussia, the eldest son of the emperor of Germany, at the altar of St. James Chapel (the same church where her mother was wed) most of London must have been running around barefoot. If the bride's magnificent gown trimmed with satin ribbons, orange blossoms and myrtle, her lace veil, diamond necklace, 18 carriages, 220 horses and more than 300 soldiers weren't enough to knock their socks off, the formal breakfast, which included a six-foot-tall wedding cake festooned with busts of the royal family, and the state banquet that evening replete with fireworks, cannons and two new stanzas of "God Save the Queen" written by Alfred Lord Tennyson were more than enough to take care of it.

All this hoopla added fuel to an already glowing fire. Ever since the queen's one-of-a-kind gown had been hauled up the aisle by a dozen train bearers to the sound of a trumpet fanfare nearly two decades earlier, the English middle class had longed for some of the royal family's glamour to rub off on their own weddings. But once they witnessed the spectacle of Princess Vicky's wedding, it became an all-consuming passion. It wasn't long before New York society, refusing to be bested by the British, picked up on the trend and spread it like wildfire into major cities all across the United States.

Today more than a century has passed since Princess Vicky traipsed down the aisle, and the world has experienced social and technological changes so stunning they could never have been imagined even thirty years ago. Yet despite time and technology we can no more let go of our image of the storybook wedding than abandon the wedding ceremony itself.

You were probably a small child when Lady Diana came down the aisle to wed Prince Charles trailing enough silk to outfit an air force battalion with parachutes. For days Americans stayed glued to their TVs, watching enrapt as the elaborate preparations got under way. It was glamorous stuff, but of course we all know the sad outcome. All the queen's horses and all the queen's men weren't enough to turn the most breathtaking wedding of the decade into a thriving marriage.

Even when you know better, there's something about the sight of lovely young people in full wedding regalia that can send you floating off into a soft-focus daydream. The problem is that when visions of turtledoves are dancing in your head you can't think very clearly. So it becomes all too easy to forget one very essential fact—the odds are very high that you are *not* British royalty! How much sense does it make to run yourself ragged and perhaps even compromise what you really cherish just to live out a tradition that isn't even yours in the first place?

One bride and groom who did just that wish now that they had incorporated some of their African-American heritage into their celebration. Not only would it have been more meaningful to them, but they would have created together something beautiful and meaningful for their community.

"We went the cookie-cutter route," the bride says, shaking her head at her own shortsightedness, "and it was totally stupid. I've given more thought to what to serve at a dinner party than I did in planning a wedding that would reflect who I am."

It isn't always easy to choose the road less traveled. The young bride who dared to express the view that she didn't want a bridal table discovered that truth when the reception hall manager nearly went into shock. But she had thought long and hard before making the choice she did, had several very good reasons for doing so and refused to be bullied by "custom." First of all, both she and her fiancé are rather quiet, reserved people who don't especially like to be the focus of attention. Second, almost everyone in their wedding party was married to or dating someone who was not in the wedding party, which means that numerous "significant others," all of whom were from out of town, would have had to sit with people they didn't know. The bridal couple felt it would be extremely inhospitable and selfish to make so many guests uncomfortable just so they could sit at a festooned table in the front of the hall like lord and lady of the manor. In choosing to say no to tradition they said yes to lovingkindness. And that is what the simply beautiful wedding is all about.

The Trouble with "Them"

As soon as you begin to feel you "have to" follow a custom because "everybody" does, you bump up against a potential problem. Perhaps the budget can't expand to include formal invitations even if you settle for thermography, which is less expensive than engraving. Or maybe you've been to enough weddings to know that you find the traditional garter ceremony not only repugnant but deeply offensive. Or maybe your church considers "The Wedding March" (from Mendelssohn's *A Midsummer Night's Dream*) secular music and says you can't have it.

All of a sudden your wedding is no longer one hundred percent traditional. Now what? Many's the bride who let one of the above scenarios or some other just like it cause major turmoil and upheaval in her life. Slavish devotion to tradition can make even the most level-headed bride come unglued over trifles that aren't worth half that much time and emotion.

Webster's dictionary defines *tradition* as "the handing down, orally, of stories, beliefs, customs, etc. from generation to generation." The bride who elected not to have a bridal table knew that her mother had had one at her wedding, as had her grandmother. Yet even before she had had time to think it through, the practice had never felt "right" to her. However, rather than arbitrarily dismiss what had been a custom for two generations, she wisely asked her mother to explain what the significance of the table had been for her.

Initially the question was met by a blank stare. Finally her mother said, "I haven't the foggiest notion. It was just something people did. I never thought about it one way or the other."

That clinched it. If there is no meaning, the young bride reasoned, then what is the purpose of passing the "tradition" on, particularly when there are sound spiritual reasons not to, given the makeup of their wedding party and their desire to be thoughtful of their guests? By having a bridal table they would have followed established custom, but they most definitely would not have been true to who they are or what they cherish.

The hallmarks of the simply beautiful wedding are creativity, lovingkindness and thoughtful preparation. In order to exercise them you have to pay close attention to your budget, your values, the feelings of those involved in your wedding and the reality of your circumstances. But you also need to pay attention to tradition. In fact, you very likely need to pay even closer attention to it than the bride who has her mind made up to have a wedding with every trimming and trapping imaginable.

What? If the idea is to exercise a little creativity and dare to be different, why ever should you care what "everybody else" is doing? It sounds contradictory, but it really isn't. The idea is not to pay slavish attention to following every tradition the wedding industry, your friends and the fairy tales say you must if you are to create a "perfect" wedding. Rather it's to take the time to consider what each custom means, where it derived from and whether or not it reflects who you are and what you believe, and ultimately to decide whether it is worth the financial and emotional cost it takes to carry it off. You may be surprised to find that some of the things you took for granted as essential are actually quite expendable, whereas others take on new depth and meaning when you begin to understand them.

What's It All About?

When tradition works—that is, when it is carefully thought through and truly reflects the personalities and belief systems of the people acting out the ritual—it can be as sweet, pure and meaningful as the first stirrings of love. But in order for tradition to be right it has to be right for *you.* That means that it must reflect in a significant way the realities of your life—who you are as an individual, as a couple and even as a family. Despite what the bridal hype would have you believe, a traditional ritual has absolutely nothing to do with fairy-tale fantasy. A meaningful ritual attempts to act out in a visible, concrete way that which is deep, true and intangible.

A fantasy, on the other hand, is something that is idealized—that is, not real. While fantasy can add charm and playfulness to your special day, it should never be confused with meaningful ritual. Fantasies are pure spun sugar—pretty, romantic, exciting and alluring but lacking in real substance. This is not to say there is no room for fantasy in your simply beautiful wedding. If you want to indulge a few whimsies, go ahead—provided of course that you know they are whimsies, are very clear about why you are choosing to indulge them, can afford them and are certain that they will cause no one pain or embarrassment. Just don't make the mistake of thinking, for example, that a bridal gown the size of a pup tent is an absolute necessity because most first-time brides elect to wear one.

One young bride who made this assumption later expressed regret that she had not followed her impulse to wear her mother's wedding dress. "I really wanted to. It fit and it was so beautiful—long, satin, studded at the top with tiny seed pearls. But I didn't because it hung very simply, had no train and worst of all, was blue. They say that blue is more for second marriages," she said.

How sad that "they" (whoever *they* are!) infiltrated something as intimate as this young woman's wedding day! Long after "they" had moved on to tyrannize the next wedding, she was left with the feeling that she missed out on something irreplaceable.

Even though she didn't take an active role in exercising it, this bride at least realized that she had a choice. Sometimes the tyranny of tradition is so subtle you don't even know you're being tyrannized until it is too late.

That's what happened to Julie, an artist whose Cinderella wedding amazed her friends who would have bet their pale pink bridesmaid dresses she would have been the last person to come down the aisle in crinolines. Julie, like her work, is bold and forthright. She is a risk-taker noted for huge striking canvases streaked with her signature color—deep purple. Yet at age thirty-one she somehow wound up walking down the aisle looking like a debutante.

"It sounds stupid, but it never occurred to me to do it any other way," she says. "I'd bought into the fantasy when I was a little kid and dragged it around for so long . . ."

"In some ways it was my fault," her mother interjects. "I think I, too, had dragged around the same fantasy for so long that it became more a matter of assumption. Of course we will buy the Princess Di dress, and of course we will have a white cake with pink roses and a plastic bride and groom on top. We didn't think. We just did it."

When you don't take the time to really evaluate your choices, you wake up one day to realize they have been made for you. Never mind that you were the one who actually plunked down the deposit for the Cinderella dress. Or even that you were the one who selected it from the rack. In the final analysis, the decision belonged to "them."

One mother-of-the-bride recalled with barely restrained glee how she said "no thanks" to the traditional white bridal bouquet when she was married in 1970. Though the florist, her mother and her maid of honor all tried to talk her out of it, she ordered a huge bouquet of daisies trailing wide yellow velvet ribbons so long they brushed the floor.

"There were plenty of raised eyebrows, let me tell you, because color like that just wasn't 'done' on the bride's bouquet in 1970," she said, her eyes shining at the memory. "But I didn't care—I loved it and I was going to have it. Every time I talk about my wedding I tell the daisy story. Obviously those flowers were more than flowers. They were my emancipation proclamation, my way of letting my family know that I had come of age. But you know what?" Here she paused and laughed. "In breaking with tradition I created a tradition. My daughter chose wide burgundy satin ribbons to the floor for her bouquet and is even having burgundy roses added to the back of her dress."

"We're just colorful women, Mom," her daughter said with a grin.

Great? Absolutely. Neither mother nor daughter allowed silly "shoulds" or "shouldn'ts" to compromise what they really wanted. Of course it's one thing to stand up for what you really believe and want when you have strong feelings about it, but what happens if you are ambivalent about a certain tradition which seems to have great significance to your fiancé, your family or your future in-laws? Sometimes by talking it over with your fiancé and your respective families you may find that, unlike the bride who said no to the bridal table, you will discover deep meaning where you thought there was none.

That was Maggie's experience. Ever since she was a little girl, she had vaguely known that the brides on her mother's side of the family placed a coin in their shoe for luck before they walked down the aisle. When it came her turn to be a bride, however, she dismissed it as a "silly superstition," one she would not carry on. But at her bridal shower she received a small box from her grandmother. Inside, resting on a piece of worn green velvet, lay a very old Irish coin—the same coin her great-grandmother had placed in her shoe back in Ireland when she'd walked down the aisle of a tiny country church in County Galway. Her grandmother, too, had worn it when she had walked down the aisle of the same ornate church in Cleveland where Maggie herself was to be married, as had her mother, three aunts and two cousins.

Holding the large coin, worth only a penny, Maggie suddenly knew that she would wear it too, not because she believed it would bring her good fortune but because it was symbolic of the deep, throbbing vein that powerfully and meaningfully connected her to her origins.

Sometimes, though, even after discussing it you may not feel especially drawn to carrying out the particular tradition your family holds dear. In a later chapter we will probe more deeply the problem of family expectations, but for now let's assume that while you are not drawn to it, you have no real aversion to it either. Going ahead with a ritual that doesn't appear to hold any meaning for you but that satisfies your family can sometimes bring unexpected blessings. Even if you don't wind up being surprised, as Maggie was, by a sudden sense of rightness and connection, there can be amazing joy in delighting those who love you.

When Mary Donna married last year, she had the same huge Italian wedding every young woman in her family has had since "the beginning of time." For weeks her mother, aunts and grandmother cooked and froze mountains of pasta pignoli, homemade ravioli, chicken tetrazzini and lasagna. They even made and decorated the traditional Italian wedding cake, a three-tiered confection which looked on the outside like the normal bakery offering "everybody" orders but inside was filled with fruit, nuts and sweet spices. Mary Donna reveled in all the traditional foods and the happy bustling about but felt ambivalent about the tradition of dancing the tarantella, a high-spirited dance, with her grandfather at her reception.

"I thought I might feel goofy or something with all my friends there," she admitted. "But it wasn't that big a deal, so I figured, oh why not? My grandparents would have been hurt if we hadn't, and they were so thrilled with the wedding. It seemed like such a small thing in the overall scheme of things that I said okay."

Unlike Maggie, Mary Donna never did feel any sense of profound meaning as she hopped and whirled around the dance floor with her grandfather, but the look of pride and joy on his face is something which brings tears to her eyes a year later.

"Whenever I remember my grandfather, I will always see how he looks in this picture," she said, pointing to a photo of a short, rotund, elderly man wearing a tuxedo and a Cincinnati Reds baseball cap dancing with a tall, slender young bride. The bride's veil is askew, and she is laughing with apparent embarrassment, but the old man's face radiates pure, unabashed pride, love and delight.

A Sense of the Sacred

Robert Fulghum, a minister and popular author, calls rituals "the frames around the mirror of the moment." Deceptively simple, this definition goes straight to the heart of it. A meaningful ritual or tradition says, in effect, "Pay attention to this moment. It's important." Whether you think them through very carefully and choose them for their meaning or carry them out as an act of love for those who do cherish them, the traditional rites that touch you most deeply are the ones that provide a sense of continuity and heighten your awareness of your passage from one state of being to another—i.e., from single woman to married woman. These rites or traditions bring you up short, make you stand back and, at least for a moment, be fully aware of the changing seasons of life.

Even though Mary Donna felt slightly foolish careening around the floor with her grandfather, she does admit to feeling a subtle sense of transformation. "I guess I felt *really* married or something," she says, groping for words. "Like 'Wow, it happened.' "

When a ritual is right and good, there is always a sense of the sacred. Even though you may be laughing and having fun (or even feeling slightly self-conscious) as you perform it, there is still a strong sense of being transported out of *chronos,* or "real time," and transported to *kairos,* or "God time."

As the bridal couple, you and your groom are the primary participants in any wedding ritual, so it is you who have the potential to be the most profoundly moved by the sacredness of the moment. But never underestimate the impact of ritual on those who come to bear witness to it. They may not be able to give voice to it. They may even feel uncomfortable with, or scornful of, calling the experience a sacred moment. But whenever a ritual arouses a deep and universal connection that transcends the ordinary, it is a manifestation of the very real presence of God. Quietly, gently, like a warm embrace, the presence wraps itself around both the moment and those suspended in it, leaving no one who surrenders to its power untouched.

Perhaps you have attended weddings and noticed married couples instinctively clasp hands or exchange private glances in church as the bride and groom exchange their vows. In that instant they are overwhelmed by the holiness of the moment, not only because they share the couple's happiness but also because it allows them to temporarily forget petty and mundane annoyances and remember their own connection to one another and the promises they too made at the altar. We need our traditions and rituals to remind us as individuals and as a community that being married is more than filing joint income tax and sharing a mortgage. We need them to remind us that we are spiritual beings deeply loved by God and deeply connected to one another.

If you have not already noticed, most of the traditions that move you to tears or fill your heart to bursting are not the ones that cost lots of money. As much as you might enjoy a hansom cab ride with a top-hatted driver and two exquisite white horses carrying you jauntily down the road through Saturday-afternoon traffic, you probably won't be affected by it on a soul level. Again, that doesn't mean that it won't create wonderful memories, but only that it could easily be stripped away without tainting the pure, distilled essence of a day filled with love and grace. When asked to name a tradition that proved meaningful and memorable, brides came up with such things as

☐ lighting a unity candle as part of the ceremony

☐ presenting each mother with a rose taken from the bride's bouquet

☐ placing a photo of the bride's deceased mother on the altar so her presence and memory might be part of the day

☐ carrying a mother's wedding Bible decorated with flowers instead of a bouquet

☐ wearing a blue topaz necklace belonging to a favorite aunt as "something blue"

☐ inviting the guests to leave their pews and gather around the altar to witness the vows

☐ a bride's "dancing" with her wheelchair-bound father at the reception to the Celine Dion song "Because You Loved Me"

None of these things cost much, if anything, in terms of dollars. None of them required elaborate preparations or huge amounts of time or stress. But assess their value against designer dresses, stretch limos and country clubs and see which side holds the most weight.

Of course there are some traditions or rituals that either aren't sacred at all or have become corrupted because the marrying couple doesn't understand their significance or chooses to ignore them and go for cheap laughs. At times these "traditions" can even be hurtful or demeaning.

Take the traditional ritual of the bride and groom feeding each other the wedding cake. Somehow an act designed to remind the couple of their interdependence and willingness to care for one other has degenerated, at least in some circles, into a competition to see who can smash the cake most effectively in the other's face. Most brides say it's the groom who seems to find this humorous, but more than one admitted that she retaliated in kind. If you have never given much thought to this bizarre practice, you may want to discuss it ahead of time with your fiancé so there will be no unhappy surprises.

"It ruined my wedding," one bride said emphatically. "I know he thought it was all in fun, and I know his fraternity buddies expected it. But it was at *my* expense. I tried not to show it, but it brought tears to my eyes."

Another "traditional" rite that trips up at least some brides is the garter toss, which is almost always performed to the sound of catcalls and suggestive music. Some brides say they never considered it a big deal one way or the other and could "be a good sport" about it, but others either opted out or wished they had. Rather than be brought up short by a "tradition" that not only has no meaning to you but might actually cast a pall over the day, explore your feelings with your fiancé and see if you can find a way to modify the ritual, find an acceptable substitute for it or eliminate it altogether.

More than one observer of social behavior has remarked on this strange juxtaposition of the formal wedding with rude, crude or lewd "customs." Why do we work so hard and spend so much money making sure that the table napkins are the same exact shade of peach as the tulips in the centerpiece and then turn around and do something more befitting a barroom than a formal setting? Some have suggested it is because formality is so unnatural to our society that we can only sustain it long enough to get through the ceremony! Mini-food fights between the bride and groom and garter throwing, these observers contend, break the tension, flip the switch and throw the party into high gear. Maybe so. But do you really want the kind of party that might be apt to follow?

If you opt for a formal wedding, you might indeed want to take a breather from the strain of doing everything "just so" and be a little more casual at the reception. Or maybe you would prefer to be a little more casual throughout the entire wedding. No problem. The *simply* beautiful wedding is more about being real than about conforming to elaborate rules and regulations concerning the way things "should" or "must" be done. Etiquette was devised as a means of ensuring civility, but it is quite possible to bend some of the rules and still treat each other, your family and your friends with kindness. In fact, sometimes breaking with tradition allows you to be even more thoughtful.

Traditionally at a sit-down dinner the newly married couple is served their meal first, followed by the bridal party and then the guests. One couple turned that tradition on its ear by asking that their guests be waited on first and they last. Another bride solved the problem of who should escort her down the aisle by asking both her father and her stepfather to do the honors. A third bride sacrificed the receiving line because her mother has arthritis and can't stand for long periods of time. Rather than embarrass her by bringing out a chair, she let the whole thing go and wound up having more fun table-hopping. And yet another couple decided to dispense with designating one side of the church "his" and the other "hers" and commingling their guests so that mutual friends wouldn't be placed in the awkward position of having to choose which side to sit on.

As you make your own wedding plans, think carefully about rites and traditions and let your heart choose its own path. In the end it matters less whether you are ultra-traditional, a trendsetter or a moderate than what criteria you use to make your choices. Remember, too, that there is one tradition that never goes out of style. It's called love. Let it light your chosen path and you will walk down the aisle, and through your life together, with grace and simple joy.

4

Room for the Groom

A m I interested in the wedding? Good question." *Steve stroked* his beard and thought for a second. "I'm going to have to go with no. Marriage, yes; wedding, no. To be brutally honest, I'll be glad when it's over. Man, it's crazy! Ever since my girlfriend became my fiancée, it's like she's got a one-track mind."

"You can say that again!" Eric concurred. "In the beginning I thought it might be cool to plan this thing, but that was before I knew what a big deal it was going to turn into. It's like no matter what we do or what we talk about, it all comes back to The Wedding. How much yakking can you do about colors, for pete's sake? Every weekend we run around seeing about this and that. It's getting to be a major drag."

Mark, on the other had, would like an opportunity to share in the decisions. "I think I might enjoy it, if anybody cared about my opinion," he said. "But every time I make a suggestion Karen and her mother look at me like I just got in from the Planet Ork."

Only Tom, the oldest member of the group, feels comfortable with his role. He and his fiancée are both in their mid-thirties. This is his second marriage and his fiancée's first. Of these four engaged men, he is the only one not planning a huge, traditional affair. Before they made any concrete plans, or even talked with wedding vendors, he and wife-to-be Carolyn jointly agreed that they had no interest in becoming yet another cog in the wheel of the Wedding Machine. They want nothing more elaborate than a small church ceremony with close friends and family in attendance, followed by a larger reception in the banquet room of their favorite Greek restaurant. No limos, no videographers, no army of attendants and especially no weighty decisions to gobble up their time, money and sanity.

"For me it's a little different," he said thoughtfully. "Carolyn and I are older and we're paying for the whole shebang ourselves, so it's not like we have all these people involved. I think it's a lot easier to keep it simple if it's basically the two of you doing it."

Tom's right. The smaller the wedding and the fewer people involved, the more likely it is that the bride and groom will share the cost and the decisions. Complex wedding plans make it less likely that the groom will either get a voice in what happens or enjoy what ensues if he does.

Traditionally the groom has been that vague, shadowy figure standing at the end of the aisle in the uncomfortable tuxedo waiting for the bride and her mother to sort it all out. Day lilies or roses? Lavender dresses or deep violet? Whatever. It didn't make a whit of difference to him. All he had to do was stay of out the way, let them hash it out and show up at the appointed time.

But all that is beginning to change. Today even in the case of large weddings the groom is moving out of the shadows and if not into the limelight, at least onto the stage. With couples marrying later in life and more grooms contributing to wedding costs, it's only natural that men want a greater say in what will happen at their weddings. Wedding protocol, too, has relaxed in response to this sociological change. A prewedding shower, for instance, might remain a women-only affair, but it just as easily might not. More and more frequently the traditional parlor games and lime sherbet punch in the living room are giving way to the barbecue in the backyard for couples.

But even though men are finally getting a voice in what happens at the wedding, several factors still conspire to keep most of their wants and needs locked in the storage closet along with the rest of the unused props, especially when it's a fairy-tale event. One of the biggest causes of this inequity is the fact that tradition has not yet completely caught up with sociology. On the one hand, we recognize that it is also the groom's wedding day, but on the other, we're such sticklers for convention we can't as a society concede that the couple should fully share the responsibilities. Tradition has too long dictated that the bride and her mother are in charge of the wedding. Although some couples have made the shift from excluding the groom to making him a key player seem almost effortless, most of the time he still doesn't quite share center stage. Which brings us to the second and perhaps most overwhelming factor influencing how the groom is treated—the old myth of the princess bride.

Bridezilla

As every little girl under the age of seven can attest, a princess is a highly exalted creature. A single pea tucked beneath a tower of Serta Perfect Sleepers is guaranteed to ensure insomnia so severe that by week's end she'll be hooked up to monitors at the Johns Hopkins sleep disorder clinic. Hands down, she is the star of the wedding, and everybody else, including the groom, is but a bit player. As one groom jokingly put it, slip a ring on her finger and the sweet, fun-loving, caring woman you fell in love with suddenly turns into Bridezilla!

Okay, so maybe that's overstating it a little. But like most exaggerations it does contain a germ of truth. When everybody agrees that you are the star, it's easy to begin acting like one. Of course you don't want the man you love to feel left out, but there is a tremendous amount of pressure on you to get everything just "right." Your mother wants one thing, you want another, and the bridesmaids threaten revolt if they have to wear anything on their heads. Just let the guy you've agreed to spend the rest of your life with suggest using hubcaps as flower containers for reception decorations and it's enough to push you right over the edge of the buffet table.

The other problem is the fantasy factor. When you've been dreaming all your life of a Martha Stewart wedding, it can be difficult to compromise. The fact is, you don't *want* to accommodate your intended's desire for gladiola because you hate gladiola and think they belong in a cemetery. And anyway, you shouldn't have to make concessions. You're the bride. It's not your job.

"Don't you want me to be happy? You know how much this means to me," one bride was overheard snapping at her fiancé at a bridal show. They were cruising the aisles in search of a vendor who could stage a balloon launch on the steps of the church after the wedding when he casually remarked that he didn't feel good about propelling pollutants into the atmosphere. From her reaction you'd have thought he'd suggested they not have the wedding. What he very likely considered to be a mild comment struck her deep-rooted sense of entitlement like an arrow making contact with a bull's-eye.

Anytime entitlement enters the picture, reason can be counted on to beat a hasty retreat. As long as you feel you have a right to your own way, you can't compromise, find creative solutions or even see that your demands may be hurtful or exclusionary. The need to control the outcome is so great that you actually begin to feel that a trifle such as a balloon launch has the power to make or break the entire day. On some level you may even realize that it isn't rational, but when you've dragged around a perfect fantasy for a lifetime, the emotional residue is like the waxy yellow buildup on the kitchen floor—it requires strong chemicals to blast through it.

Of course it isn't necessary to be snappish or argumentative like the bride in the above example to make your fiancé feel like excess wedding baggage. Mark's comment that his fiancée and her mother regarded him as an alien life form every time he offered an opinion points out the truth that brushing off suggestions as though they were annoying flakes of dandruff and not taking the time to listen to the feeling behind the suggestion can be every bit as hurtful and dismissive as outright churlishness.

Like many men in his position, Mark has given up trying. He figured it just wasn't worth being shot down again and again. For some grooms it isn't a big deal whether they play an active role in the wedding plans—in fact, some may not even want one—but Mark genuinely feels left out.

Even if your fiancé doesn't have passionate feelings about where the reception will be held and whether to offer a vegetarian entrée, how you respond to his minor suggestions at this important time of your lives can set the tone for future communication. Planning your wedding together is a priceless opportunity to learn how to listen attentively, negotiate, compromise and come to an agreement without either of you smoldering with unspoken resentment.

In order to make room for the groom, however, it may be necessary to first talk with your mom. With convention on her side she may have a difficult time sharing her role of wedding planner with her future son-in-law. But if you can lovingly explain that while you very much want her help and input, you also feel that the wedding is an opportunity for you as a couple to test your ability to work together effectively, she may prove surprisingly cooperative. As long as she doesn't feel that her role has been usurped, it's less threatening and can be even appealing to help you begin the process of joint decision-making. Instead of helping just you her role becomes one of helper, confidante and role model to both of you.

"If You *Really* Loved Me . . ."

As you begin to work together as a couple, it helps to remember that only a very small percentage of what you communicate is said with words. Silence, body language, meaningful looks and sighs can often say more than angry or dismissive words. Very often in your zeal to make sure everything is "perfect" you can find yourself using one or more of these to subtly control the situation even when you say that you welcome your fiancé's ideas.

One groom remarked that he could always tell when his bride-to-be didn't like his input because she invariably folded her arms and offered a noncommittal "mmmmm" to what he was suggesting. Learning to read one another's nonverbal signals is definitely part of the process of communication. But when you aren't upfront about differences of opinion, it's impossible to deal with them effectively. You may easily get what you want now, but you are planting dangerous seeds for the future. Plant too many and eventually you'll reap a bumper crop of communications problems.

One of the biggest factors contributing to communication difficulties is the old myth that if someone loves you they automatically know what you really mean whenever you express even the most veiled thought. In fact, they know you so well that you don't even have to express anything! You just think *Aruba* and—bingo!—your fiancé is down at the travel agency booking the trip. No matter how many times psychologists warn us that life works that way only in paperback novels and three-hanky movies, we still cling tenaciously to this dangerous romantic notion even when we know from sad experience that it's guaranteed to bring us grief. At this period of your life together you're especially vulnerable to it because everything is still so new and fresh. In the throes of romantic love the myth seems not only believable but practically carved in stone.

"If you really love me, you'd know," you say when he fails to understand why you are angry about his choice of ushers.

"If I have to tell you, it doesn't count," you shoot back when he asks what he can do to plan a romantic honeymoon.

While it's certainly no fun being the one uttering these statements, try being on the receiving end of them! The recipient feels confused and helpless, knowing that from here on in the chances of doing or saying the right thing are about zip.

Even after years of marriage most couples never reach a magic pinnacle where they automatically anticipate the other's every need before a word is spoken. To think you can do it so early in a relationship is like believing it's possible to reach up and grab a handful of the sky. Sure there are times when your partner will anticipate and meet your unspoken wishes—when they happen these times are small, perfect miracles—but most often you will have to share your desires and points of contention honestly and lovingly before you can reasonably expect fulfillment.

But what happens when you are completely straightforward about your own feelings and your partner is equally straightforward with the opposite opinion? How can you negotiate when he wants what he wants and you want what you want? One way to begin is by asking (without hostility!) a simple, one-word question—*why?* Why do you want that particular band? Why don't you want to wear a morning coat? Why is it so important that you change the date of the wedding so your cousin can be a groomsman? Very often the request is not as arbitrary or inconsequential as it may seem initially when all you can see is your fantasy falling apart around your feet. While it may be hard for your partner to answer—he may not know himself why he does or doesn't want something—if you are attentive and in control of your emotions you can begin to pick up clues that will lead you to the emotion behind the words.

One bride told the story of how her fiancé kept insisting that they not have the wedding too late in the day, despite her repeated explanation that she didn't want a lot of lag time between the service and the reception. When she finally asked him why it was so important to have it early, he shrugged, looked at the floor and mumbled, "I don't know. It just seems like a good idea in case we wanted to do something else."

Finally—a concrete clue. The words "do something else" told her there was more at stake than simple stubbornness. With a little gentle probing she eventually unearthed the real deal. It seems he wanted very much for them to visit his grandmother in the nursing home so she could see them in their wedding finery but was reluctant to suggest it for fear that such a sad setting would cast a pall over the festivities. Fortunately, his worries were unfounded. Once his fiancee homed in on the truth, not only was she happy to accommodate it but she went so far as to suggest that they have the bakery make a decorative single-layer wedding cake to bring with them so that his grandmother and the other residents could share in the day. By taking time to listen to the motivation she not only honored the man she loved but brought joy to many others in the process. That's what the simply beautiful wedding is all about!

There may, however, come a point where you don't agree about something you both consider major and can't, no matter how hard you try, find a compromise that works. There is no question that somebody has to concede, but who will it be? If only one of you feels strongly, the decision is easy. The one who cares less backs down and waits until something weightier presents itself before taking a stand. But when the issue is equally important to both parties, it can become so emotionally charged it sends off sparks.

Though you probably won't believe this when you're in the throes of it, you have actually been handed a blessing! A major disagreement is an opportunity to see how you behave in a crunch. It gives you a chance to test your generosity, your sense of fair play and even how well you express gratitude.

One young couple reached an impasse over table decorations. The groom, who kept several aquariums of exotic fish in his apartment, wanted goldfish bowls filled with—you guessed it—bright orange goldfish swimming around green plastic palm trees. The bride was appalled by what she called "the unbelievable tackiness." She had her heart set on candles in glass globes trimmed with ribbons, baby's breath and miniature roses. But no matter how hard she tried to convince him to abandon the goldfish idea, he remained adamant.

"We reached the point where I began to feel like it wasn't about goldfish anymore," she recalled. "It was like he had to win no matter what. Even after I agreed to go along with the idea provided we get a florist to help us find a way to artfully display them, he said no. They had to be plain old goldfish bowls. It was so controlling, so angry and stupid."

Ultimately this young woman had second thoughts about going ahead with the marriage. When she said the argument wasn't about goldfish bowls, she was right—her "red flags" had been activated by the feeling that his need to win was always paramount. If goldfish bowls could create this much dissension, she reasoned, what would happen when the disagreement concerned something vital like a child or a job change? Once she thought about it, she began to see that the same intractable behavior had been present when he had insisted on choosing the engagement ring by himself, when he decided to look for an apartment for them in a specific neighborhood and when he insisted she not take a job she knew she would love in favor of one that paid more. Wisely she postponed the wedding and insisted they get counseling. Whether or not they marry depends on whether they can overcome a very serious obstacle in their relationship.

Another young couple resolved their differences much more graciously. Susannah and Todd had their first significant argument over something a little weightier than goldfish bowls, but how they handled it showed a maturity lacking in the above scenario. Susannah wanted to be married in her childhood church, while Todd felt strongly that being married in the chapel on their college campus made more sense. They had met on campus in their sophomore year and had countless friends there, and the school was equidistant from both of their families' homes. In this instance compromise seemed out of the question. All they could do was hold the wedding in one place or the other or else come up with a third location that didn't appeal to either of them.

"At first I was pretty upset," Susannah admits. "Then I realized something. We both have ties to campus, but I'm the only one who feels nostalgic about St. Luke's. While I wasn't 100 percent happy about letting go of the old fantasy of walking down the aisle where I'd walked so many times as an acolyte, it did make sense that I should be the one to give in this time.

"And Todd was so happy! He thanked me over and over again. It was such a joy to have been able to give him his wish. He in turn told me to choose where we would go on our honeymoon and we would go there, no questions asked. I chose Williamsburg, Virginia, and he didn't bat an eyelash. I think it was pretty fantastic."

To be able to bring joy to the one you love and show heartfelt appreciation for an act of selflessness is indeed "pretty fantastic." It has nothing to do with being a doormat either. It's about thoughtfully choosing who has the stronger case and what is best for the relationship. Very likely the outcome of the next impasse will go in the bride's favor because this couple understands that the idea isn't to keep score but to honor each other, God and the love with which they've been richly blessed.

As you work out the difficulties of conflicting wants, meditate both alone and together on the beautiful words from St. Paul's letter to the Corinthians, "Love is patient and kind; love is not jealous or boastful; it is not arrogant or rude. Love does not insist on its own way; it is not irritable or resentful" (1 Corinthians 13:4-5). Let them slowly become part of you and watch the transformation.

Please, Can't We Talk About Something Else?

One of the toughest parts about making room for the groom is the fine line you walk between involving him enough and involving him too much. Although he may enjoy interviewing disk jockeys and tasting the caterer's gourmet creations, even the most involved groom doesn't want to make wedding planning a full-time occupation. As Eric and Steve both pointed out in the opening discussion, a little planning is fun, but too much grows staler than week-old wedding cake.

You too can quickly get burned out if you spend all your free time doing nothing but looking at fabric swatches and fretting over details. You're a multifaceted woman with a job or college to finish, family, friends and many other activities and interests. Why would you want to put your "real life" on hold for a year or more while you endlessly work and rework the plans for a single day? You also have a fiancé to consider, a man who loves *you,* not your ability to orchestrate a wedding.

Engaged couples can easily hit a bump in the road when wedding planning becomes the focus of the relationship. Even when it involves him in the planning, endless wedding talk can make your fiancé begin to feel that you are no longer so much interested in *him* as you are in all the busyness. Soon he begins to feel more like the vehicle that makes it all possible than a person who is dearly loved for who he is.

Your engagement lasts for a long time—and it is becoming increasingly longer in direct response to the Wedding Machine and the quest for perfection. The average engagement is now eighteen months, and often longer than that, for the simple reason that it takes a great deal of time to pull off the "perfect" wedding. With more and more couples waiting in line for the same reception sites and services, you have to plan far in advance if you hope to book your first choice.

One bride mentioned that she went to look at a reception hall feeling slightly embarrassed that she was shopping so early: she didn't plan to be married until after her college graduation, which was two years away. Much to her amazement, the manager whipped out a calendar and showed her that two weddings had already been booked in the month and year she had chosen!

Eighteen months or more is too long to be single-mindedly focused on wedding, wedding, wedding. Even the most interested groom does not tend to be as involved in wedding planning as the bride. While you are whirling through a world of details and appointments, he is still grounded in "real life." Unless you make time to join him there, you cannot possibly hope to connect. Once the excitement of the engagement is over, this period can be a very lonely one for the groom, who often feels as though he has lost the person he loves most to a world he neither understands nor *wants* to understand that intimately.

The other problem with nonstop wedding planning is that it can become a convenient smokescreen to cover up problems in your relationship that need immediate attention. As long as you get along great when you're busy auditioning soloists for the ceremony, you never have to confront the fact that you have very different ideas about what you want for the future. Grooms, too, can eagerly buy into all the excitement and "specialness" of being in the limelight—sometimes as much as brides can. More than one couple has put heart and soul into planning a wedding so perfect it rivals those in the color spreads in the bridal mags only to wake up when it's over asking plaintively, "Is this all there is?"

One couple told the story of a wedding they attended only eleven months ago which they estimated rang in to the tune of at least thirty thousand dollars. As they watched the elaborate preparations get under way and saw the bride and groom cooing at one another as they basked in the glow of attention, they felt a little envious of all the glamour and romance. Compared to their friends' plans, their own wedding, and even their relationship, seemed conventional and—well—maybe a little staid. Not anymore though! Six months after the newlyweds ran out of the church through a cloud of soap bubbles, they filed for a dissolution.

Come to think of it, there is a marked similarity between the words *dissolution* and *disillusion*. When life doesn't turn out "happily ever after," the couples with few coping skills and the shakiest foundation are first in line at the courthouse.

Don't fall in love with a role! You are both so much more than bride and groom. In the whole drama of life these are actually very minor parts. You may get to wear the fanciest, most expensive costume you will ever wear in your life to perform them, but when the curtain comes down at the end of the evening, the show is over and real life begins. There's something very hollow and sad about couples who get stuck in wedding mode. Anyone who follows the wedding chat on any one of the numerous Internet wedding sites can soon pick them out. They are the couples or individuals whose weddings have been over for months but who still hang around endlessly debating the pros and cons of having a tea dance!

Even if there are no serious underlying issues in your relationship for wedding fever to conveniently mask, constant, intense focus on plans and expensive finery robs you of precious unencumbered time to be doing other things. One young couple, Jeannie and Ed, decided to use part of their engagement period working together at an inner-city youth center. Every afternoon when they are finished with classes (they are both college seniors), they walk the five blocks from campus to a center where kids pour in after school. Jeannie and Ed read stories, help with homework, play games, break up fights, plan holiday parties and, most of all, talk to troubled, disadvantaged kids about the possibilities of a different kind of future.

"It's definitely brought us closer," Ed said. "We walk home and talk about how Devon is doing and how we seem to be making progress with Yolanda's pinching habit and on and on. We have a purpose that's bigger than we are."

"That's not to say we never talk wedding or that we're some kind of saints," Jeannie added with a laugh. "I squeal over pictures of wedding dresses right along with my sorority sisters. And Ed and I have had fun making decisions. But we are more than the wedding."

Another couple used their year-long engagement to open an import business together, while still another built their first home, a log cabin they purchased as a kit and put together themselves with only the help of occasional subcontractors. Of course it's not necessary to leap into a major project as these couples did to use your time well—projects can sometimes cause the same sort of problems excessive wedding planning can. What matters is that you strike a comfortable balance and not lose what brought you together in the first place.

It's also important to note that there are some conventional grooms who really have little interest in wedding planning. If yours is one of them, bombarding him with swatches of fabric and price lists is not going to rev up his orange-blossom hormone. Brides who handle underinvolvement with grace say they can do so because they have made the distinction between interest in the wedding and interest in the marriage. All of them felt confident that they were loved and that their fiancés were eager to marry them. Knowing that, they could happily set about making preparations for the wedding with friends and family who shared their enjoyment of the process.

As one bride put it, "What difference does it make whether he does this stuff? I fill him in on the things I think he might care about and let it go at that. Like I asked him if he wanted a groom's cake. He didn't know what one was, so I explained it and he thought it was pretty neat. He's having a chocolate cake with a football motif. I think it's the only thing he chose out of the whole wedding, which is completely fine by me."

Because she felt secure in their relationship, this young woman felt no compulsion to drag her reluctant groom-to-be over a mountain of minutiae. Brides who do not feel as secure, however, sometimes try to draw their men into every aspect of the planning in the mistaken hope that involvement will somehow clinch the deal. Instead it can bring about the opposite outcome—the men retreat further, often becoming distant emotionally. If you know that your fiancé's reluctance to flit from photographer to photographer in search of the most artistic portraits is caused not by disinterest in you but by discomfort with all the planning or even a basic feeling that one professional photographer is as good as another, making room for the groom takes on a whole different meaning. Instead of finding ways to make him feel more involved, your task becomes one of honoring his choice *not* to be.

But whether yours is a man who enjoys debating the merits of caterers or one who would rather wash the car, one thing remains a constant. Making room for the groom always means putting your relationship and your marriage ahead of wedding planning. A simply beautiful wedding, after all, derives its charm from a simply beautiful relationship.

5

Making Peace with Perfection

There's a wonderful wedding scene at the end of the movie *Sense and Sensibility*. After their marriage, Marianne Dashwood and Colonel Brandon run out of the church through a throng of well-wishers and climb into an open carriage. All around them village children, waving multicolored silk ribbons tied to the end of long poles, laugh, shout and shove against one another in an effort to get closer to the wedding party. Excitement shimmers in the air as they wait for the red-jacketed groomsman to toss a handful of coins in the air. The silver disks arc heavenward and for one perfect moment hang suspended like tiny halos of radiant light against a sky as blue as the heart of a hydrangea blossom.

"That scene could have been my wedding," sighed Caroline. "Well—for a little while anyway," she amended with a wry grin. "We were riding down this winding country road in a horse-drawn carriage away from the prettiest little white-steepled church, and people were throwing carnations in our path. I remember thinking to myself, *This is a scene straight out of Jane Austen.*"

Greg, her husband of two years, laughed. "Yeah, until it became a scene straight out of Stephen King!"

Less than an hour after their arrival at the bride's grandmother's country home where the garden reception was to be held, a line of severe thunderstorms blew in without warning. As the wind whipped ferociously and hailstones the size of marbles pelted them, the wedding party, the caterers and even the guests scurried around grabbing the punchbowl, platters of food and armloads of beautifully wrapped gifts. Before they could get everything safely indoors, the white marquee tent collapsed, and the top tier of the wedding cake belly-flopped into the goldfish pond. As she stood at her grandmother's kitchen window watching gift cards sailing like seagulls across the lawn, Caroline was sure that her perfectly planned wedding had wound up an unfixable disaster.

"I was appalled," she recalled, "But there was no time for hysterics. Eighty-five people were waiting for me to get it together. My gown was totally sopped, so the first thing I had to do was change. Fortunately my aunt lives next door, so she ran over and got me a nice pink cocktail dress of my cousin's. My grandmother threw a lace cloth on the dining-room table and rearranged the food, most of which was okay. Then we took her corsage and my mom's and used them to make a new top for the remaining layers of the cake. For a while there it was pretty crazy, but once I got past the shock it actually turned out to be fun."

"Yeah, we had a blast," Greg agreed. "People really loosened up. And you oughta see the video!"

If you're shuddering at the thought of such a scene, much less the video of it, you have plenty of company. When it comes to wedding disasters, this one definitely rates a spot on the A list! Fortunately most calamities are calamities only to the bride (and maybe her mother). Guests rarely notice last-minute flower deliveries, a misspelled name on the cake or a flower girl who wanders off the altar. And if they do notice, they smile kindly, commiserate and tell you it doesn't matter, it was lovely anyway. Most of the time they mean it too. Small mistakes make you seem human and approachable. The more elaborate the wedding, the more distancing it can be, especially to those who are uncomfortable with pomp and ceremony. But make a tiny mistake, or react to one with grace and good humor, and suddenly there's an almost palpable sense of relief. "Aaaah," the crowd seems to say, "that ethereal white-gowned creature with the perfect hair is only 'our Julie' after all!" Not that that helps much during that awful moment when the cake collapses. Your stomach clenches. Your heart pounds. Tears prick your eyeballs like needles. And something inside you folds in on itself, as though the air were being let of out of your very soul. In the slick, perfect pages of the bridal magazines, disaster simply doesn't happen. Cakes stand firmly and beautifully on their pillars, rain stays in the sky where it belongs, grooms don't fumble the vows, and brides never ever get zits on the their chins the morning of the wedding. How, when you planned it all so carefully, could something possibly go so wrong?

Believe it or not, the crushing disappointment wedding mishaps bring is not really about cakes, the weather, zits or grooms who mix up the vows. It's about transformation. While the coins are in the air catching the glint of the sun, they're jewel-like and magical. The second they hit the ground they become just coins again, hard, scratched and ordinary. It's the same with your wedding. When you are riding in the carriage through the flowerfall with the sun shining and the good wishes of your guests wafting around you like music, you are a princess on your way to happily-ever-after. But just let the wheel of the carriage fall off the side of the road, and suddenly you're jarred into the realization that you are still *you* living in an imperfect world where mistakes can and do happen, no matter how carefully you plan.

Of all the mistakes you can possibly make in planning your wedding, the most glaring is thinking that perfection is a worthy goal. It's like sending an engraved invitation to disaster. Perfectionists tend to see the world in shades of sharp black and white—things are either perfect or horrible, with no middle ground. As soon as the first thing goes wrong, perfectionists fly into a tizzy, not realizing that such a reaction opens the door for even more tension and upset.

The fact is, no matter how spectacular everything looks in the magazines or how well organized you are, there are some things over which you have absolutely no control. You can't govern the weather, wish away human error or predict how everyone will act or react at any given moment.

When you want more than anything to believe that you can achieve perfection by the sheer force of your will, it's easy to forget the one thing you don't see in all those glamorous photos in the wedding magazines—the blood, sweat and tears that went into producing them. Many rolls of film are shot, scenes are set and reset, flowers are misted, models are combed, powdered and airbrushed, and sometimes food isn't really food at all but plastic facsimiles. You, on the other hand, only get one chance to experience your wedding day. There are no retakes. How well you handle mishaps, both large and small, depends on your ability to roll with the champagne punch. Some brides, like the one in the above example, seem to do it almost effortlessly, while others allow even the small stuff to give them an old-fashioned case of the vapors.

Maureen was one of these high-strung brides. The second she woke up to the realization that her wedding day was going to be marked by torrential rain, she came unglued. The church lacked a dressing room, which meant that she had to race across the parking lot shrouded in umbrellas while three people trailed behind carrying her train. Once they were in the vestibule, things didn't improve. An "anchor" flower fell out of her bouquet and refused to go back in. The crowd seemed sparse in the enormous church. The organ sounded "tinny." During the ceremony the best man had to leave the altar to retrieve the ring because he had forgotten to get it earlier from the bride's father. And later the groom's grandmother held up the photography session by talking too long with an old friend, which meant the wedding party was fifteen minutes late getting to the reception. There Maureen took one look at the food, catered by a local club, and deemed it "horrible."

Maureen snapped at the caterer, cried in the limo and at one point threatened not to walk down the aisle at all. After her cousin suggested she "grow up and get over it," she spent the remainder of her reception sulking in the ladies' room. Three years later she calls her wedding day "an unqualified mess."

There are, of course, two ways of looking at these two totally different scenarios. You could say that Caroline showed maturity and Maureen acted like a spoiled, self-centered prima donna. Or you could say that Caroline is so unreal she ought to be nominated for sainthood, while poor Maureen did what any bride worth her bustle would have done under the circumstances. There were thousands of dollars at stake, not to mention countless hours of planning and preparing. Who but the most heartless curmudgeon would begrudge a disappointed bride the privilege of a little biblical teeth gnashing and rending of garments?

Both women spent more than ten thousand dollars on their wedding, and both paid for a large part of it themselves. Both also planned for more than a year and strove to set a perfect scene. For Caroline that meant creating a Victorian fantasy (never mind that Jane Austen is Regency—she was shooting more for mood than historical accuracy), while to Maureen perfection conjured up black and silver sophistication. Yet despite the fact that both brides expended an equal amount of time, money and creativity, when the glamour bit the dust, only Caroline, who had actually suffered the greater loss, was able to get a grip. What made the difference?

The Choice Is Yours
Certainly it can be argued that some people seem to take life's minor mishaps in better stride than others. Human behaviorists have noted that even in infancy some children are casual and laid-back while others get edgy any time the slightest change is introduced into the environment. But temperament is only part of the story. A big component of your wedding well-being is how deeply married you are to the notion of perfection. If your standards are so rigid that you can't accommodate the flower girl's getting a last-minute case of the weepies and not being able to walk down the aisle or the florist's calling to report a shortage of calla lilies, you build an even stronger case for simplicity than the bride who holds less stock in flawlessness!

The fewer the number of players, accouterments, details and rituals, the less chance you have of being stressed out and disappointed. Who wants to spend such a happy occasion tied up in knots over trivia? Even the fussiest brides who say their weddings went off without a hitch (or almost so) have admitted that after it was over they wilted like snapdragons, exhausted and relieved, as though an enormous burden had been lifted away. It had been impossible for them to relax and have a good time because the compulsion to keep an eagle eye on the proceedings overcame enjoying the moment.

There's a charming old custom that oddly enough is embraced by at least three totally disparate cultures. Iranian rug weavers, Navajo rug weavers and Amish quilters all create their art with humility, believing that only God has reached the state of true perfection. Since no artisan can hope to compare to divine perfection, they acknowledge their own human frailty by creating a tiny flaw on purpose and hiding it somewhere deep in their work where only the most discerning eye can find it.

This is not to say you need to sabotage your own wedding, but only that it is wise to realize that the only burden you have to be perfect is the one you place on yourself. Plan well, be creative, and then place your wedding day in God's hands, knowing that no matter what happens he will create from it something beautiful. Perhaps it will not be exactly the "something beautiful" you had planned and dreamed of. Maybe it won't even be close. But no matter what happens, peace is found in knowing that "there is a purpose for all things under heaven."

One bride loves to tell the story of how a quirky accident at her wedding brought about a happy ending she could never have imagined. When the four-year-old ring bearer tripped on his way up to the altar and fell, sprawling, on the marble steps, he immediately let out an anguished howl. Quickly one of the bridesmaids dropped her bouquet and rushed to pick him up. Seeing that the ring pillow had cushioned his fall and he was more frightened than injured, she gently carried him down to his dad, a widower, who was grateful for her quick intervention. The next year the bride at the first wedding found herself on the altar again—this time to witness the vows of her ring bearer's father and her bridesmaid.

Even what may seem at the time like the most horrible happening of all can prove to have a purpose that may not be visible until later. Such was the case when one of the worst wedding nightmares imaginable occurred to a young woman from New York City. She made headlines when her groom abandoned her at the church the day of her

$100,000 wedding. A bride with less grace and charm might have behaved very badly and have even been forgiven for doing so. But this young woman borrowed the jacket from a relative's ensemble, buttoning it and wearing it as a dress, and then bravely and graciously invited her guests for hors d'oeuvres at the hotel where she had planned to host her reception. Only later, when she had time to recover and reflect, did she realize that in that moment of utter humiliation and sorrow was hidden a very real blessing—she had been saved from making the wrong choice in a mate.

It is an extreme example, no question. The odds are high that nothing even remotely that calamitous will happen to you. But the point is, if you believe that God is the heart, the mind and the soul of both your day and your life, you don't need to try to control your wedding minute by minute. You can relax and meet whatever it brings with complete faith. More than likely all of your mishaps will be tiny ones—unless of course you choose to turn them into huge, glaring gaffes. How you handle disappointment is always a choice. And the choice you make sets the tone for the rest of the day.

Stage Sets and Casting Calls

Relinquishing thoughts of perfection does not begin, however, the moment you wake up and realize that the day you have so long anticipated is finally at hand. It begins back at the very beginning, at the moment you decide what kind of wedding you will have. If you insist on making perfection your goal, you will not only set yourself up for anxiety and disappointment but also run the risk of creating a day that seems to your guests more painstakingly staged than a Broadway revival of *My Fair Lady*.

One bride and groom who come from a blue-collar, meat-and-potatoes background went all out to create a society reception, only to have their guests feel so out of place they all cleared out en masse as soon as they'd survived the ordeal of figuring out which fork to use for dinner! Another bride hired a wedding manager to run around making sure everything went according to plan. But the endless fussing with table decorations and the stream of orders barked at the club's staff became so off-putting that the guests felt as though they'd walked onto the sound stage of a soap opera instead of into a real-life party.

"There's something a little desperate about it," one bride-to-be said of the need for perfection. "It's like you're trying too hard. Like people will think less of you if your wedding doesn't live up to some phoney-baloney standard."

Wise words. When you are comfortable with yourself, there is no need to try to impress anyone. If something goes a little wrong, you laugh, pick up the pieces and move on, knowing that nobody really cares anyway. Guests come to your wedding because they love you and want to share in your joy. Sure, they enjoy oohing and ahhing at all the unaccustomed glamour, but they certainly don't want to be held hostage by it. They are there to have a good time.

Not long ago one of the cable channels, Home and Garden Television, ran a program about wedding planning that shed light on an interesting truth. Immediately after a wedding, guests were quizzed on the steps of the church about the floral arrangements inside. How many had there been? What color were they? What kind? Almost no one could answer with any certainty, and very few responded correctly.

How often have you yourself gone to a wedding and brought back only impressions of the overall effect and mood? You know it was formal. The bride wore an ivory dress with a cathedral train. The brides-maids wore hunter green. The decor was gold and ivory. The meal was a buffet, the food fair, the band wonderful. And that's it. The fact that the napkins had been folded like swans and the bridesmaids' lipstick exactly matched the pink of their nails totally escaped you. The fact is, most of the time spent agonizing over tiny, insignificant things is time, energy and emotion wasted.

Not only does the drive for perfection squander precious moments and make you crazy, but it invariably makes everyone around you crazy too. More than one bride has lost friends after her wedding for the simple reason that she treated them like actors at a Broadway "cattle call." Or worse yet, excluded them because they didn't live up to some false notion of perfection.

One bride, to her deep regret, decided not to ask one of her dearest friends from college to be in the wedding party because at the time her friend was suffering from a hormonal imbalance which had caused her face to break out with particularly virulent acne.

"It was incredibly petty and mean," she says, looking back. "I'm ashamed to think I was capable of it. But all I could think about at the time was the way everything would look. The pictures are forever. You can't fix them. I had hired this art photographer (it cost a fortune) and he did a fantastic job. Trouble is, the perfect pictures aren't so perfect because when I look at them all I see is that Suzi isn't there. It really caused a major rift in our friendship. I guess we're still sort of friends, but not like before."

Even when you don't do something that extreme, you can still unwittingly hurt the people you love by making demands that may seem like no big deal to you but may be a very big deal to them. One bride insisted that all the bridesmaids wear their hair in the same upswept style.

"Everyone looked great but me," her younger sister recalled. "Keri knew I have thin, fine hair that won't stay up, but she insisted I had to do it anyway. All day I felt so ugly and dumb. I couldn't stand being there. It really hurt that she would care so little for my feelings."

Another bride made the common mistake of putting too much financial pressure on her attendants. It was bad enough that she chose a gown that cost a third more than she had told them to expect and then demanded that everyone buy a costly pair of navy linen shoes. But when she insisted that every woman had to buy the same pair of twenty-dollar hosiery, two of her friends revolted.

"Twnety dollars for pantyhose!" one of them squawked. "Like someone's really going to notice. She says they have a silvery sheen to them. I don't care what they have. I'm not paying twenty dollars for pantyhose when I can barely afford everything else, and now she's talking about us all having our hair and nails done at the same place the morning of the wedding so we'll all have the same lip and nail color. Like we're Barbie dolls or something. This has definitely gone too far."

Few brides deliberately set out to cause hurt feelings or strained budgets. They just want to set a lovely scene and get carried away in their effort to do it.

This is something you need to guard against from the very beginning. The best way to do that is to listen to what your attendants tell you about their preferences and finances. The fact that they have agreed to be in your wedding is actually a gift to you, not just an honor *you* have bestowed on *them*. Too many brides don't get this part. Largely that's because the Wedding Machine is geared to the notion that the wedding should emulate the royal court—the bride as princess and her attendants as ladies-in-waiting. You may never have thought of comparing the modern wedding with antiquated court customs, but think about the weddings with which you are are familiar and see if you can't see this notion being played out in the behavior of the bride.

It helps to remember that being in a wedding requires a significant financial outlay, not to mention a huge expenditure of time. Bridesmaids usually pay for their own ensemble, attend showers and luncheons given in honor of the bride (and provide all appropriate gifts), attend the rehearsal and rehearsal dinner, and help the bride on the day of the wedding with everything from getting dressed to staying calm. By being a considerate bride you show your bridesmaids that you realize what you are asking of them and that you appreciate the fact that they have agreed to make your day special.

One bride sacrificed perfection to make every one of her attendants comfortable and wound up with a charming and unique wedding. Because she had a large wedding party composed of women who wore everything from petite to plus sizes, she solved the dress style problem by saying that each attendant could wear a pastel gown of her own choosing. The only requirements were that each dress be tea length and not the same color as anyone else's. The women enjoyed making their own selections and appreciated the fact that they didn't have to overspend and could select a dress they might actually wear again. There were no hurt feelings, squabbles or embarrassing moments, and the effect was as fresh and pretty as a garden of summer flowers. Plus they had fun shopping and modeling their selections for one another.

Of course this is not to say that you have to totally surrender your own desires to please everyone else. Sackcloth and ashes, however artfully arranged, don't make for a simply beautiful wedding! It's your day, and you and your fiancé deserve the right to make the final decisions—which means that there may be times when you want something that proves unpopular with one or more members of the party.

That's exactly what happened to a couple who yearned to have a medieval wedding, authentic right down to the lack of utensils on the dining tables. Once the wedding party got over the initial feeling of embarrassment at having to wear costumes and pretend to be living in the Middle Ages, they accepted the fanfare with good humor—that is, until the maid of honor found out she was expected to get to the church on horseback.

"I'm deathly afraid of horses," she said. "As much as I care for my friend, there was no way I was going to get on one. I thought she might be mad at me or say I couldn't be in the wedding, but she was great. She and her fiancé talked about it and decided I could walk alongside the bride's horse. I don't feel like they're unhappy with me at all."

This bride and groom successfully persuaded their friends to step out of their safety zone by approaching them with good humor and flexibility. They still got what they wanted—a medieval wedding—but the maid of honor also got what she wanted—both feet firmly planted on the ground! Better yet, the wedding was not one whit less "authentic" or lovely than it would have been had they created a ruckus over something as inconsequential as who would be on horseback and who wouldn't.

The odds are good that your friends are equally willing to make concessions for you as long as they feel you care about their feelings and appreciate their efforts. There's hardly a woman on the planet who hasn't donned her share of hot pink taffeta horrors in the name of friendship.

The Perfect Audience
Moving past the pitfalls of perfection doesn't stop with how you treat your wedding party. It also includes how you regard your guests. Too often they tend to be considered part of the tableau, the perfect hand-picked audience to applaud your script, costumes and stage set.

Again, most brides don't set out to be hurtful. They simply get caught up in the trap of trying to orchestrate a day of unparalleled elegance, and somehow that quest seems to justify excluding those who might "spoil" the ambience.

Many brides draw the line at children for exactly this reason. Admittedly cost can be a factor if you are hiring a caterer, as children don't tend to eat much, and at twenty dollars or more per plate their meals can really wreck havoc with the budget. But creative brides have gotten around this impediment by asking the caterer for a price break for kid-sized portions. One couple did something especially creative. When their caterer proved unwilling to provide kiddie meals, they arranged to have carry-out food brought in for their younger guests. Kentucky Fried Chicken proved infinitely more popular than chicken cordon bleu anyway!

But the truth is, cost is only one reason children are excluded from the festivities, and very often not even the major one. Children are messy. Loud. Unpredictable. They wail right at the moment you promise to love and honor, spill soda all over the tablecloth and hop around the dance floor getting in the way of the other guests. But they also add charm, spontaneity and joy, and look adorable in the pictures.

How you feel about having children at your wedding is a personal matter, but it's a good idea to consider the question very carefully before making a decision about whether or not to invite them. If you are not prepared for the unpredictable, definitely don't ask them to be in the wedding party. Very often little ones get invited to participate just because they are cute and the "perfect wedding" wouldn't be perfect without an adorable little moppet to carry the rings and scatter the rose petals. But children aren't pint-sized mannequins to be dressed up in frilly dresses and suits with short pants and then blamed for spoiling the day if they don't live up to your expectations. A considerate bride takes that into account beforehand. If you know your tolerance for unexpected surprises is low, you may actually be making the kinder choice if you decide not to have children, either in the wedding party or as guests.

Before you decide, though, consider what is the usual custom in your family. Will family members be hurt if their kids are excluded?

Carla is a bride who failed to take that into consideration and wound up creating more bad feelings than she'd bargained for. Cost was the main factor in her choice to say "no kids," but she had also chosen a smallish hall and felt that with kids running around it might get too crowded and chaotic. Unfortunately she had not taken into consideration the fact that her extended family includes its children in all family celebrations. When the aunts, uncles and cousins heard the no kids rule, they sent back their response cards with regrets. Two years later there are still rumblings about it.

Kids, of course, aren't the only ones who can be excluded in the quest for perfection. One bride admitted to not wanting to invite a mentally challenged uncle, while another says she wanted to exclude most of her father's side of the family. When asked why, she responded, "Because they're so embarrassing. They don't know how to dress." What's interesting is that she admitted that were it an "ordinary" celebration, a birthday party or a Fourth of July picnic, she would not hesitate to put out the welcome mat. But in her mind a wedding is a rarefied event that only the crème de la crème of one's family, friends and acquaintances are privileged to attend.

By the same token guests can also be treated like commodities when they are invited precisely *for* their cachet. Many's the bride who has extended invitations to people she barely knows just to be able to drop the "right" name. When planning your guest list you can never go wrong if you list the people who love you and have made an impact on your life. As one bride said, "If you wouldn't feel comfortable inviting someone over to watch a video or have coffee, then why would you invite them to witness something as intimate as your wedding?"

Not Perfectly Matched

If ever there were two words that don't go together as cozily as *love* and *marriage,* they have to be *perfection* and *creativity*. The minute you seek perfection when you are in the throes of creating anything— be it a novel, a painting, a new accounting system or a wedding gown—you might as well halt the process because you have effectively tethered your imagination to a post and said, "I am giving you this much leash and no more." Nothing paralyzes you faster than trying to do something letter-perfect. Who hasn't had the experience of wanting to make something, say a ceramic pot, and settled down happily to the task only to be told that your effort wasn't "right"? "You needed to shape it like this, color it like that." Suddenly it wasn't fun anymore.

Perfectionistic behavior is also isolationist—it cuts you off from the fun and ideas others can provide in the planning stage. Perfectionists are not open to suggestions because they are convinced they are the only ones who can carry off the project flawlessly. This also means that even when they are acting on their own ideas they find it impossible to relinquish control and delegate tasks to others who might enjoy participating. Then, when the stress goes through the roof, they complain that nobody wants to help!

The best way to find creative wedding ideas and solutions is to brainstorm with family and friends. You don't have to act on every idea you get. Just say thanks, jot it down, and see if something jells later. By asking the people you love and trust for their input and help in carrying out plans, you go a long way toward alleviating some of your own stress while making them feel needed and appreciated.

If you feel sick every time you have to make a decision about your wedding, think about how driven you are to be perfect. Very often that compulsion is what keeps you from moving forward with any sense of confidence. Some brides get so fearful of making a mistake that they can't make any decisions at all. So rather than put a deposit on the location they really want, they dither around from reception hall to reception hall until all the prime sites are booked and they have no choice but to settle for second best. Others make fast decisions only to wind up second-guessing them. Johanna was one of those brides who keep looking back over their shoulders.

"I picked out my dress and immediately saw a better one in a magazine," she admitted with an embarrassed smile. "So I stopped the order on the first one and lost two hundred dollars on the deposit. Then I ordered the second one at a different shop and began to think maybe the first was better after all. I very nearly canceled *it*. Actually I would have if my parents hadn't put their foot down. It all seemed so overwhelming."

The reason wedding planning seems huge and overwhelming is once again our unrealistic thinking about weddings. When you're caught up in the idea that whatever you pull off had better be perfect or else you forfeit what could have been the happiest day of your life, it's no wonder you feel panicky. There are so many choices, and the Wedding Machine keeps cranking out new ones. How are you supposed to know which is "best"? The truth is, there is no "best." There is only what is right for you—what you like, can afford and feel comfortable adding to your day.

Before you begin to shop for your wedding, it's wise to know what kind of look you're aiming for. Will it be Victorian or contemporary, formal or casual? Or perhaps something totally unique? The answers to these questions will narrow down the number of goods and services from which to choose. Once you have an idea what you want, draw up a budget and begin scouting out what is available. When you hit upon something which feels "right," trust yourself enough to go with it. *And then stop shopping.* Continuous looking will only fill you with self-doubt and add to your frustration. It also helps not to take along an entourage when you make decisions. The more opinions, the more confusing decision-making can become.

There will always be people who don't admire your choices, just as there will always be people who get a better idea than you had or who find a new way to do the same thing you did. The good news is, wedding planning is not a contest! What matters is that you choose as wisely and well as you can, relax and have fun doing it. Use your imagination, be playful and spontaneous, and forget about what the wedding gurus tell you you "have" to have.

The best way to do that is to redefine perfection. A "perfect" wedding is one where you exchange vows with the person you have committed your life to, join with friends and family in happy celebration, and create a warm, wonderful memory to treasure for a lifetime. Anything else is just icing on the cake. Buttercream or fondant? Who cares? Either way, it will be simply beautiful.

6

From This Day Forward

Their eyes shone as they told the story.

"I still can't believe it! We fell through the cracks," the bride crowed. "We got out of going to the premarriage thing at the church!"

"The old minister was leaving and assumed the new guy would take care of it, and the new guy thought the old guy already had. We didn't bother to advise him any differently," the groom added with a satisfied smile.

They don't know it yet, of course, but they have just been cheated. By not getting any premarital preparation, this couple missed out on the opportunity to

☐ openly discuss issues they might not have considered, discern differences and express their deepest feelings in a safe, caring environment

☐ learn how to resolve issues fairly and cleanly without being a doormat, having to be right at all costs or sweeping unpleasant topics under the carpet

☐ examine the role models each of them had for marriage and learn how these different styles of interacting complement or challenge each other

☐ spend quality, reflective time focusing solely on each other with no outside interruptions

☐ explore the sanctity of marriage and connect on an even deeper level

So much for trying to outsmart the church, huh?

Ordinarily this is not a couple who are easily swindled either. Had the caterer failed to give them the promised two-hour, two-visit consultation, you can bet the only crabs at the reception would not have been the ones on the buffet table. But they are more than willing to be shortchanged by their church as long as there are no hitches in either the rehearsal or the ceremony. At twenty-seven they feel confident that they are mature enough to know what they are doing and resentful of any requirement to "go public" with the private details of their relationship. They know that nearly half of all divorces occur within the first three to five years of marriage, but they insist that the statistic has nothing to do with them. They have their bright shining future drawn finer than a Rand McNally road map.

Chances are you are not this negative about the marriage preparation requirement. Studies have shown that those who are active in their church and feel a sense of belonging there welcome the opportunity to learn more about one of the most pivotal relationships they will ever enter—or at least don't balk quite as loudly at the prospect. Yet if you are like most brides and grooms working your way through the stress and excitement of planning a wedding, there's a good chance you haven't given much thought to the process of premarital counseling. In part that is because of how you feel. When you're caught up in the wild enchantment of romantic love, it is hard to believe there will ever come a day when you don't feel exactly as you do at this moment. Even though you know there will be problems, you are confident that you will handle whatever life brings fairly and amicably.

Perhaps you have even demonstrated that already. With engagements lasting much longer than they have in the past—a year to eighteen months is average, but many couples are together four years or more before saying "I do"—the odds are high that you have leaped over some pretty significant hurdles together. Maybe you were separated by college or military service, survived a breakup and reconciliation, experienced a death in one of your families, or even confronted such serious issues as drug and alcohol abuse. You feel ready to make a lifelong commitment and are confident that you have the right stuff to meet whatever challenges real life dishes out. You can hardly believe that a few sessions with a counselor or a couple of classes can offer anything you haven't already heard or learned the hard way from experience.

Actually all this talk about marriage preparation may even make you feel slightly queasy. What does it entail? Will it be embarrassing? Will you be put on the spot? What happens if you start probing too deeply and end up *causing* problems rather than curing them? Everybody has heard stories of couples who went for counseling, opened up Pandora's proverbial box and wound up breaking up. Who wants to risk that?

Then there's the matter of time. You don't have any. Every minute is taken up with work, school and a zillion wedding details. As soon as the wedding is over, you tell yourself and your perhaps lonely fiancé, there will be plenty of time to focus on each other again. But for right now you are in charge of planning a major event. The last thing you need is one more stressful thing to add to the mix when you already feel like you have taken up residence inside a pressure cooker.

Believe it or not, your mixed feelings of confidence, romantic love, hesitancy and stress are only part of the reason for your skittishness about church-required marriage preparation. The second and without question most crucial factor is the deafening silence from the Wedding Machine. Bells peal, the organ cranks out "Here Comes the Bride," glasses clink and the crowd cheers, but barely a word is said about how to use your engagement as a time of reflection and learning. Judging by the beautiful wedding planning literature you have been pouring over for months, it would be easy to surmise that it is far more difficult and important to learn how to properly address your invitations and figure out how many sets of sheets and towels you require than to plan how you will live the rest of your life. There are two reasons for this.

The first goes straight back to our cultural fantasy. Who wants to face hard, cold reality in the midst of sculpting a dream out of blocks of ice, bolts of silk organza and bushels of hothouse flowers? To talk about divorce statistics, conflict resolution and effective communication at such a romantic time seems a bit like throwing cold water on the bright flame of the beautifully beribboned unity candle. Second, marriage preparation is not yet a big business, though it could become one if states begin to require mandatory premarital counseling as a condition for acquiring a marriage license. In 1997 legislatures in at least eleven states began debating the issue, and already the U.S. military is "strongly encouraging" its enlistees to attend marriage education classes, even if they have already tied the knot.

However, until premarital counseling moves outside the parameters of the church, you are not apt to see much attention paid to the topic either in the books that tell you how to turn your fantasies into reality or in the glossy pages of the bridal magazines. Magazine advertisers like to see editorial copy that boosts consumer demand for the products they have to sell. At this point those products are gowns, diamonds, invitations, honeymoons and household goods—not long-term marital contentment.

Changing Times

All of that may be about to change, however. Many of today's twentysomething brides and grooms have lived through their parents' divorces and know firsthand the havoc divorce wreaks on children. While they yearn for permanence, love and companionship, they most emphatically do not want to repeat the mistakes of the previous generation. Though they are not eschewing marriage—and in fact may even be reversing the trend toward later marriages—they are, in some cases, seeking out psychologists for premarital counseling before they ever show up on the doorstep of the church. Hopefully you share their desire to take a hard and honest look at your relationship. Hopefully, too, you understand that if you let it, the Wedding Machine will lure you away from one the most important jobs you will ever undertake.

Callie and Tom are one couple who understand this so well that they have struck out on a course that might be viewed by some as either overkill or an indication that they have serious underlying problems and should not be getting married at all. But the fact is, they are closer than ever and are looking toward the future with optimism and confidence. At age twenty-three they know that they are among the youngest of today's crop of brides and grooms, a factor that is not in their favor. They know that the fact that both sets of their parents have been divorced is another major strike against them. Yet they feel deeply connected to one another and want to make a lifelong commitment. They also want to do everything they possibly can to minimize the risk.

"Would you believe that you can actually buy wedding insurance?" Callie asks. "I mean, you can get a policy that will pay for your photos to be retaken if something goes wrong—stuff like that. We consider what we're doing to be *marriage* insurance."

What Callie and Tom are doing is taking an advanced course in relationships. Their journey began back in their senior year of college, when they hit a snag in their relationship and sought guidance through their university's free counseling service. Now, with the wedding only six months away, they have signed up for a weekend seminar in addition to the individual counseling and pre-Cana program required by the Catholic church where they will be married.

Someday they hope to be able to give back to the church what they are getting now by becoming either a team or mentoring couple and sharing their experiences with others preparing for marriage. Because of their commitment to education, they also agree that they would not hesitate to seek help should the need arise after marriage.

"You'd go to a doctor if you had the flu, right?" Callie asks. "So what's the difference between that and consulting a professional if your marriage gets a touch of flu? Marriage is hard. There's no shame in admitting you need a tune-up once in awhile."

Make no mistake about it—the time you spend preparing for your marriage will pay back dividends far greater than the time you spend on your wedding. You are about the begin the most important and longest-lasting relationship of your life. Even becoming an effective parent is grounded in how well you interact as a couple. The style in which you approach life issues together affects not only you and your children but even your children's children! It is an astonishing thing to think about, but couples in crisis very often got that way by repeating destructive family patterns that have sometimes existed for generations.

Crazy as it sounds, the fact is, we sign up in droves for classes on how to buy a house, invest our money and fold flowers from origami paper—and willingly fork over vast sums of money to do it—but until very recently we have never even considered that relationships require education too. Fortunately we are living in a time of exciting opportunity, as both church and government officials are not only speaking out about the need for quality marriage preparation but actually taking steps to see that it is readily available to you. In 1995 the Council on Families in America, in a report to the nation, urged churches and religious organizations to establish and strengthen premarital counseling. With 87 percent of all marrying couples choosing a church wedding whether or not they actually belong to or attend church, this is prime positioning for such programs, since it makes them readily available to the vast majority of engaged couples. Churches have heard the call and have begun responding in ever more creative ways.

But the availability of quality programs is only half the battle. The second half is taking advantage of them. This is tougher than it sounds, because the Wedding Machine is working overtime to convince you that the glut of goods and services it offers is the end-all and be-all for the attainment of happiness. But the truth is, while it may provide you with exquisite floral arrangements and a cake too gorgeous to cut, the Wedding Machine will not help you get the deepest wish of your heart—to love and to be loved for a lifetime. Only *you* can help ensure that by making the decision to allocate the bulk of your time and energy toward marriage preparation.

Shopping for Services

Wouldn't it be great if marriage came with a lifetime warranty or a money-back guarantee? Unfortunately the only papers you are handed at the end of the ceremony are the license issued by the state and your church's certificate of marriage. However, today's premarital programs are so effective that they are as close to a warranty as it may be possible to get. Of course no program makes you totally divorce-proof—marriage is an ongoing process that requires continuous work and education. But some researchers maintain that after a couple completes a program that utilizes the newest and best tools available to counselors, it is possible to predict with 90 percent accuracy which marriages will make it and which will fail to go the distance.

Unfortunately not all programs are state of the art, which means that you, the consumer, have to take charge of seeing that you get the highest quality available. If your church offers only the most cursory preparation, then it may be necessary to look into additional programs such as Engaged Encounter, which began as an offshoot of the Marriage Encounter program, or Marriage Savers, the brainchild of syndicated religion columnist Mike McManus. One couple reported that the church they were attending required only two meetings with the minister—one to go over the service and make sure they understood it, and the second to map out the music! Fortunately they were being married in the bride's home state, and the minister there refused to accept such shoddy preparation.

When Tammy and David got married two years ago, they paid the required four visits to their pastor but left feeling unsatisfied. Though they were planning a Protestant wedding, they decided that since they had been hearing good things about the Catholic Engaged Encounter program, they would enroll. It seemed like a natural fit. Not only did they have family members who had attended and come back giving it high marks, but they also had family members who had participated happily in Marriage Encounter, a similarly formatted program for the already wed. At the time of their marriage they were twenty-eight and thirty and had been together for two years. Because their pastor felt they were good candidates for marriage, he had not subjected them to any more than the most routine counseling. They arrived at Engaged Encounter with both a sense of confidence and a high degree of expectancy. They were looking forward to spending quality, uninterrupted time together and were very eager to do the work. This was not the case with some of their fellow participants, however.

"We noticed that the younger the couple, the less they gave to it," Tammy commented. "They would laugh and snicker, whisper to each other and even read magazines! But we really enjoyed it. The great thing is, it's just between the two of you. You get to write and talk on a variety of topics. I found it very helpful because, unlike most women, I don't feel comfortable sharing my feelings. David is very romantic, very open, very good at that, and it's hard for me to keep up. But through this weekend I learned that I can share myself and that he will listen. We didn't learn anything new about each other necessarily, but we did learn a valuable skill to take away and use in the future."

If you are a savvy shopper when it comes to hiring the best caterer for the price, don't you owe it to yourself to ferret out the very best premarital program you possibly can? Such a program may be available free, or for minimal charge, through your church, but even if you have to pay for additional counseling, this is one line item you will be happy to have included in your wedding budget. Of course, the most pressing question is, what should you look for when you are "shopping" for marriage preparation?

One of the largest studies of premarital counseling programs, conducted between 1987 and 1993 at the Creighton University Center for Marriage and Family in Omaha, Nebraska, offers some insight. Forty thousand couples participating in premarital counseling programs in the Roman Catholic Church underwent scrutiny to determine their attitudes about counseling before enrollment, how they felt about it after completing the program, and what type and intensity of program proved most effective for them. What researchers discovered was this:

□ Counseling is by far most effective when it is done at the very beginning of a marriage. Within the first year 93.8 percent of couples found it rewarding and helpful. By the second year the perceived efficacy had dropped off to 78.4 percent, and it continued on the same steady decline in subsequent years.

□ Whether couples attend counseling because they are required to or because they choose to is immaterial in terms of perceived value. After completion of the program, both groups reported it to be a valuable experience, although those who went in with the highest expectations did report that they got more out of it than their low-expectation counterparts.

□ Couples agreed that the most effective format is a team approach as opposed to an individual one-on-one meeting with a pastor. Ideally, they say, this team should consist of couples in successful long-term marriages, clergy and other church staff. They emphasized, however, that the clergy definitely added to the overall success and that they would not want a program that excluded them.

☐ The topics considered to be the most helpful were the five Cs: communication, commitment, conflict resolution, children and church. A sixth, career, was viewed as less helpful, but this may change as the number of dual-career couples continues to grow.

☐ Couples definitely equated intensity with perceived value. A single session was deemed of poor value, but so were too many sessions. The ideal was felt to be around eight or nine sessions—almost three times the number stipulated by churches requiring only the bare-bones minimum!

☐ There is a strong statistical correlation between the perceived value of marriage preparation and prior formal religious education at the high-school or adult level. Those who underwent such education were much more predisposed to the idea of learning about marriage and took away more from it than those who had none—which means, of course, that premarital programs should not be stand-alone offerings but an integral part of overall lifetime religious education.

One valuable tool in widespread use by more than twenty-five thousand U.S. churches and counseling centers in conjunction with other more interactive forms of preparation is a written survey called Prepare. Created by social scientist David Olson and his colleagues at the University of Minnesota, it asks the prospective bride and groom to independently indicate their agreement on a scale of 1 to 5 with 165 carefully crafted statements. If you are already thinking it sounds like one of the love quizzes you take for fun in women's magazines, think again. Likewise if you count yourself among those who have talked about "everything." Chances are good that you haven't fully considered such nuances as "I expect some of our romantic love will fade after marriage."

Once you have completed the surveys, they are sent to the University of Minnesota to be scored. What you get back is not a pass-fail, letter grade or percentage but a detailed report indicating your strengths and weaknesses. Counselors who use Prepare can then help you work on potentially troublesome areas or, if your overall score proves dangerously low in all areas, help you decide what to do next. The originators of Prepare are gratified by the fact that 10-15 percent of couples who utilize it decide to break their engagement, sometimes even before the results are back from Minnesota. The survey brings up issues that get them talking, and very often they realize themselves that they are headed down the wrong path. Others choose to postpone the wedding and seek more aggressive counseling. Either way, they are enormously fortunate to have had the chance to spot potential trouble before they wound up making a mess of their lives and the lives of their future children.

As scary as it may seem to consider that your engagement could be called off, it helps to remember that no one is going to tell you that you can't get married. A good counselor may advise postponement, but he or she will always respect your right to decide for yourselves. Premarital counseling is not an adversarial us-against-them situation. In fact, it is much the same as talking with a consultant about your wedding. Both the wedding consultant and the marriage counselor are there to help you get what you want with the least amount of pain.

Another useful new marriage preparation tool is the use of mentor couples. These are successful couples who have been married at least ten years and who undergo training to help them share what they have learned via a one-on-one relationship with an engaged couple. What's exciting about this concept is that it provides an easy, open forum to talk freely, not only about the future but also about what you may be feeling right now. Our cultural myth feeds us the sweet little lie that the engagement period is a time of pure bliss, despite the fact that experience usually proves otherwise. Talking with a trained couple who have lived through the same problems and emotions you are feeling can be wonderfully reassuring. Very often it is also considerably less stressful than sharing intimate thoughts with family members or friends during such a pressured time.

One of the best-known programs utilizing the mentoring process is Marriage Savers, but of course there are others. Marriage Savers trains its mentoring couples for an amazing twenty-six weeks. These couples use a prepared test to help you assess your compatibility and then meet with you a minimum of six times. Their track record is most impressive, and they are continuing to expand into numerous states. If your church does not have information available, the group has its own home page on the Internet.

There are, however, numerous variations on the mentoring theme, and there are apt to be more as the concept becomes ever more widespread. One program in Texas, run by a psychologist in private practice, stands out from the pack by mentoring its mentors. In other words, the couple who mentor an engaged couple also have mentors of their own with whom they meet on a regular basis to talk and confront difficulties. Their mentors do for them what they do for their couples—walk them through a seven-step process designed to deal with issues, offer support and encouragement, keep them on track and pray with them for successful resolution of problems. The underlying premise here is that even in high-functioning marriages problems will continue to crop up and require attention—a fact that is useful for you to know as you begin your life together.

Cold Feet and Wedding Jitters

For most young couples, marriage preparation means confronting the future. While that is certainly a big piece of any such program, it is not the only one. A good program will also help you deal with something our society jokes about but that is not all that funny when you are the one experiencing it. Call it "the jitters." Call it "cold feet." But whatever you call it, it is upsetting, to say the least. How do you know whether what you are feeling is normal or whether it is a warning signal you need to pay attention to?

As every counselor will tell you, no one is completely immune to nagging questions about the rightness of impending marriage, no matter how much in love they are. Marriage requires you to leave all that is safe and familiar and leap into the great unknown. It's a little like standing on the end of the diving board in those final seconds before you relax your toes and free-fall head-first into the deep. Will you make it safely? Will you do it with style and finesse? Will it give you the pleasure it seemed to promise? And even more basically—will you survive the experience?

Sometimes feelings of fear and insecurity wash over you in waves throughout the engagement period, and sometimes they hit in one scary blast right before the big day. Either way, they often come as a bolt out of the blue—amazing, unsettling and more than a little frightening. You felt so confident the night you said yes to the proposal, the fact that you are second-guessing yourself *now* catches you off guard. The dress has been ordered and the hall booked. Maybe the invitations have been ordered. Maybe they've even been sent. Your mother will have a conniption if you tell her you want to change your mind—if, that is, you really *do* want to change your mind.

It is perfectly normal to question such a major life decision. It is also normal to feel scared and vulnerable, fear a loss of identity, and wonder whether you are too young or too inexperienced to make a major commitment like marriage. It's normal, too, to wonder whether you will be a good spouse or a good parent, whether the person you love will love you unconditionally forever and whether the differences between you will grow like kudzu vine into a thorny, impossible thicket you can never hack your way through.

It's even normal to wonder whether there is someone else out there who is your perfect soulmate, if only you will wait long enough for him to show up! Almost everybody feels one or more of these things at some point along the way even though they may be afraid to admit it, even to themselves.

The problem is, when you are busy moving down the conveyor belt of the Wedding Machine, you and your fiancé may not be traveling along hand in hand. The pressure of planning a wedding, the differences between you that wedding planning seems to highlight, and the typical underinvolvement of the average groom all conspire to add a level of stress to your relationship that probably wasn't there previously. Consequently, your feelings of closeness may wane from time to time, often sounding alarm signals. Sometimes this sense of distancing even resurrects old issues you thought certain you had already resolved.

Distancing is unpleasant whenever it occurs, but during your engagement it can be even more unsettling because you still have a chance to question your decision.

Here is where premarital preparation can pay off big dividends fast. By talking through your complex feelings with your fiancé and your counselor or mentoring couple, you will learn something that will stand you in good stead for the rest of your lives together—how to restore intimacy following the inevitable periods when you feel less connected. Anne and her fiancé Gordon made this happy discovery when, unbeknownst to each other, they both came down with a massive case of cold feet right before the wedding.

"I was fine until about a week before the wedding, " Anne recalls. "But all that week I kept waking up in the middle of the night agonizing over whether or not I was making a mistake. Every time anybody asked anything about the wedding that I perceived as pressure, I about snapped their head off. I even fantasized about telling my parents I didn't want to go through with it."

"It hit me about midweek," Gordon says. "Anne was so cranky, and I felt like she was constantly mad at me for not helping enough with the wedding. And then I got to thinking that maybe we hadn't known each other long enough, and that led to worrying about possible career clashes if one of us got transferred. By Thursday of that week I was a total wreck."

What saved the day was the last-minute appointment they had with their counselor. Because they were married at a church in a town where they don't reside, they had had a difficult time getting to their appointments and had been forced to schedule the last one the day before the rehearsal. When they showed up at the agreed-upon time, their collective tension was so intense they were practically crackling with it. Immediately their perceptive minister helped them talk openly and honestly about their fears.

"We talked for a while, and then he had us go into two different rooms and actually visualize telling each other we wanted to end our relationship," Anne says. "He told us to forget about the money and the guests and our parents and all that kind of stuff and just think about what it would feel like to call off the relationship—to actually walk through it in our imaginations. What we would say. Where we would say it. Giving back the ring, walking away. Being alone again. About five minutes into it I was sobbing."

"Oh wow, yeah," Gordon says. "When he put it like that everything fell away except Anne. I could see as plain as day it wasn't Anne I was uptight about but the whole wedding thing—the stress with our families and the money. We left that office feeling closer than we had in months."

That is the power of a good preparation program and a great counselor. Choose one with whom you feel a sense of rapport and commit yourselves to spending the time and doing the work it requires. Chances are good that beautiful things will begin to happen.

7

Pictures for a Family Album

Move in closer, Mom. Put your arm around the bride, Dad. There, that's it! Everybody smile now!"
Click.

A family photo for your wedding album. You will repeat this scenario countless times with every possible configuration of your family and your fiancé's. But when the pictures are developed and mounted in the white leatherette album, what will you see when you look at them? Behind the bright smiles and fancy clothes what will lie lurking in the shadows—months of squabbling and dissension, or a time of joy leavened with a bit of the tears and tension necessary to complete the process of beginning a brand-new nuclear family?

If you answered neither, you are very likely going to be surprised by what ensues over the next several months. Your upcoming marriage is a season of great joy and celebration, but it is also a time of massive change and upheaval. To expect that there will be no family conflict is about as unrealistic as thinking you can have a "perfect" wedding! Unless you are fully emancipated adults, living out of state and planning and paying the entire cost yourselves, chances are good that you will experience some—uh—difficult moments as you try to integrate your respective families and somehow pull off the wedding of your dreams.

This is not to frighten you into tying your bedsheets together with Girl Scout knots and beating a hasty exit out your bedroom window but rather to help you deal with some of the unexpected tensions that spring up in the course of planning even a simply beautiful wedding.

While you are basking in the rosy glow of romantic love, your family is in the process of being changed forever. No matter how happy they are for you—and hopefully they are delighted—a wedding signifies three universal things guaranteed to bring a lump to the throat of not only moms and dads but often younger siblings as well:

☐ the inevitable passage of time

☐ the final step in the process of your growth from child to adult

☐ a hole in the family circle that will never again be filled in quite the same way

Some families struggle less than others with these issues, but it is a rare one that does not encounter a sense of loss, confusion and upset. Families who tend to talk through their problems honestly and straightforwardly usually handle wedding stress very well. They understand that tension and emotion can cause upheaval and don't become unduly alarmed when difficulties spring up. Once the sparks stop flying, they regroup, talk through what they are feeling and work out a solution. But the majority of families muddle along doing the best they can—which means that very often you are the one caught in the line of fire. When it is too hard to talk about painful feelings, those closest to you very often act out their emotions in ways that can seem baffling, if not downright annoying.

Your sister feels envious because you are getting married and she doesn't even have a boyfriend. Rather than express how left out and isolated she feels, she turns the simplest issue into a battleground. She hates the dress you select for the bridesmaids. Gets miffed because you want your best friend to be maid of honor. Pouts when you tell her she has to be escorted by the groom's "geeky" brother. It's enough to make you seriously consider running away from home! But before you start fantasizing a destination wedding (a trend which, by the way, is growing) in Hawaii, Fiji, Scotland, Tibet—or anywhere else your bickering, squabbling, frustrating family is *not*—take heart. Though it may not be possible to come through totally unscathed, there are ways to calm the natives and keep the tribal fires from burning down the village.

The *Big* Picture

The first thing you need to know to survive the storm is this: understanding is everything. When you know why these people who love you are yanking you, and to a lesser degree your fiancé, back and forth like a tug-of-war rope, you can protect yourself from snapping into two frayed pieces. Not only must your family adjust to changing times and changing roles, but they are also being asked to adjust to an onslaught of new people who very likely have different expectations, different temperaments and a different worldview from their own. The two families may even come from different social, cultural and religious backgrounds. Of course all of these differences can create wonderful life-enhancing diversity, but they can, and very often do, become the source of continuous conflict, especially as long as anyone (or everyone) feels threatened.

Will these new people with their strange ways steal you away from them? your family wonders. Will they influence you or (God forbid) change you in some horrible, unfixable way? Will they monopolize all your time? Will they be kind to you? And if they are kind, will you come to love them more than your own family? Then there is the question of Aunt Josephine and Uncle Ralph—what will they think about your marrying a Catholic?

If all of these questions seem preposterous to you, try to imagine yourself in your family's place. You get to choose to begin a whole new exciting phase of your life, but they don't get to choose anything. Not only do they feel as though they are losing you, they also have to live with the results of your choice. So they make demands and issue ultimatums—not to hurt you but to assuage some of the anxiety. Controlling such trivialities as the flavor of the wedding cake and who will stand where in the receiving line feels a whole lot better than whirling around in the center of an emotional tornado.

The second thing that causes families to act in unbecoming and hurtful ways is the fact that the marriage of a child resurrects old issues. Parents who divorced when you were a teenager are suddenly catapulted back in time not only to the pain of the breakup but to the time before that when, like you, they were filled to overflowing with love, wonder and hope for a shining future. For some parents this creates the fear that your marriage will end up the same way theirs did, while others get so caught up in their own pain they never make the connection. Either way, though, the old baggage resurfaces and gets played out in such issues as who will walk you down the aisle and who will pay for what.

Third, your wedding can make your parents feel a strong need for control if they have a high stake in what it represents—that is, if they see your marriage and wedding as a reflection of their financial status, taste and success as parents. It isn't all that hard to imagine how money-conscious parents can get alarmed when their only daughter announces she is having a small wedding with cake and punch in the fellowship hall after the service. It is not even too much of a stretch to understand how a mom who sees herself as the arbiter of style and design would come a little unhinged when her daughter wants to walk down the aisle sporting a nose ring. But how on earth can a daughter's wedding possibly reflect on anyone's ability to be a good parent?

One young woman found this out the hard way. The day after she announced her engagement, her normally calm, collected parents immediately spun into a frenzy of telephoning, shopping and planning. Almost from the start every decision evolved into a skirmish, which invariably ended with somebody (usually the confused and frazzled bride) reduced to tears. But it wasn't until a knock-down, drag-out, full-scale war erupted over the wording of the invitation that it finally dawned on her what was happening. Her parents saw the wedding as their final parental act. How they pulled it off would, in effect, be the definitive statement of what kind of people they were and what sort of values they had instilled in their daughter. Moreover, it would be a testament to the strength and closeness of the family unit.

Never mind that in their frantic desire to get everything right, they failed to notice that by treating their daughter like an inept child they were actually distorting the truth and projecting the very image they were trying to avoid! All they could see was the need to do this thing "the right way" no matter what it cost them, both financially and emotionally. In their minds, "good" parents raise perfect daughters who make a wise choices, marry in their childhood church and follow the mores, customs and traditions of the family to the letter.

Finally, there is the issue of the passage of time and what this means to your parents. On the one hand, your wedding assures them that they have successfully done their job raising you. But on the other, they are filled with a bittersweet nostalgia for the child who once was, tinged with the painful realization of their own mortality. As one younger mother of the bride commented, "Every time somebody uses that expression 'mother of the bride,' I look around to see who they're talking about. How could it be me? It seems like only yesterday I got married myself. To tell you the truth, it makes me feel kind of sad, like it's all happening too fast. Before you know it, I'll be old. I can hardly fathom it. And it scares me."

As you can see, your family's vulnerabilities are painfully close to the surface. But difficult though they are for you to contend with, they are not the only things you need to consider as you try to make sense of the tension that may be surrounding you as plan your wedding day. While your relatives are whirling around in their own private tornado of emotion, your fiancé's family may well be doing some pretty fancy whirling of their own.

They are about to "lose" a son and in the process gain a whole passel of strangers whose ways may not be their ways. They too have standards and convictions they want upheld, insecurities and old issues that bring them pain, and worries about what other people will think about their son's choice of a wife. Sometimes the cause of these feelings is deeply buried, but the feelings themselves are right on the surface where they can cause nice people to behave in not-so-nice ways. Typically your in-laws pull in one direction and your parents respond by yanking in the other. Rather than confront each other directly, both sides tend to use their adult children as intermediaries.

"Tell them we absolutely cannot take one person off our list," the groom's mother urges him.

"You are just going to have to tell him that we cannot afford to go over one hundred meals, and since we're the ones paying for it they need to make the cuts," your parents respond.

What is being tugged around here, of course, is your loyalty. Who, you ask yourself, does it belong to—your families or each other? This issue will be discussed in greater depth a little later in this chapter, but first let's take a look at the most central figure of wedding planning—your mom—and what your wedding means to her.

Mother Knows Best

It was a busy Saturday afternoon in May at a lovely upscale bridal salon, the kind of old establishment place that has been outfitting upper-middle-class brides for generations. A tiny young saleswoman staggered under the load of heavy gowns encased in thick plastic that were being piled one atop the other as though they were sheets of paper in her arms.

"We'll try both of these too," a beautifully coifed middle-aged woman said decisively, adding two very ornate white ballgown-style dresses onto the load.

"But Mother . . ." her daughter ventured.

"When can we get a fitting room?"

The bride looked pleadingly at the saleswoman. "I want to try the short-sleeved ivory too," she said softly.

"Sure," the young woman replied from behind the plastic bags. "Let me just get rid of these and I'll be back for it."

"No need," the bride's mother snapped. "She will be wearing *white*."

Ouch.

Unfortunately this is not an isolated scene. Twice more during the same visit to that salon the very same scenario played itself out with variations on the theme. In one case the bride, a tall, attractive woman in her late twenties, actually took out a tissue to dab at her eyes.

What causes mothers to behave as though they were the ones getting married? Why do they have to spoil one of the happiest times of your life? The reasons are as varied as mothers themselves, but one thing is certain: whether your relationship with your mother is close, distant or downright adversarial, problems can and probably will develop. That's because despite the condition of your relationship, the bond between you and your mother is as ancient and primeval as wind, water, earth and fire. Your wedding is the backdrop against which you choreograph the most difficult of all dances—the dance of separation.

Not only must your mother struggle with all the complex emotions already mentioned, but she is also forced to wrestle with the fact that, like it or not, you are a grown woman heading into a world to which the gates are barred to her. Try though she might, she cannot follow you into your marriage.

Perhaps from the very day you were born she has harbored a fantasy about your wedding day. In her mind's eye you are captured in an illusion of white like a beautiful fairy princess—a perfect manifestation of all the dreams, hope and love she holds in her heart for you. When your own vision conflicts with that long-held and deeply treasured image, it jars her with a reminder that you are an individual, a person separate from her with your own thoughts, dreams and opinions. For her it is a frightening thing to contemplate.

If circumstances or finances did not allow her to have a "real" wedding of her own, or if she chafed under the thumb of a controlling mother herself, her feelings may be even more intensified. Suddenly your wedding represents a chance to recapture her own girlhood dreams. A few mothers dust off sad memories of deprivation and find the determination to allow their daughters to make their own decisions—in fact, they are so conscious of it, they often hesitate to offer an opinion even when one is requested! But for most mothers the struggle to let go is ongoing, difficult and painful, even when they want with all their hearts to accomplish it. In part that's because the cultural icon of the princess bride is as deep in the marrow of their bones as it is in their daughters'.

Whose Wedding Is This Anyway?
So what does all this mean? If you are thinking that you have to accept everybody else's desires for your wedding whether you like it or not, relax. You don't. This is not a lesson in how to be a doormat but rather a call to compassion.

When you refuse to get caught up in the grinding gears of the Wedding Machine, you have the luxury to stop and think about how the people who love you might be feeling. You also have the opportunity to allow your love and joy to spill over and soothe some of their pain and anxiety.

There is no question that your wedding belongs to you. You deserve the right to express yourself and make your own selections so long as you don't ask your family for anything that exceeds their ability to provide. But along with that basic right comes a distinct set of responsibilities, including the responsibility to treat both your family and your fiancé's family with respect at all times—even, and most especially, when they are making life difficult.

Very often it costs very little to be gracious. Aunt Judy suggests you serve salmon mousse at the reception. You have no intention of dong so. But rather than make a federal case out of an inconsequential thing, you simply smile sweetly and say, "That's a unique idea. We really will have to consider that. Thanks for thinking of it." Then you note it in your wedding planner so she can see and leave it at that. It's a small thing, a simple thing, but when you respond this way she feels heard and appreciated. It is only when you are frantic to make everything perfect and are full of your own "stardom" that you feel the need to snap, "No, thank you! I hate salmon mousse and so does everybody else!"

Admittedly it is much easier to be gracious over small matters with people who are not intimately connected with your wedding than it is with those whose wants seem more threatening, but this is a very real place to begin. Small acts of kindness have a way of multiplying. Others will notice your graciousness and emulate it, and before you know it, what you extended will come back to you sevenfold.

If you see right from the beginning, however, that your family feels compelled to take the reins, you may need to have a heart-to-heart talk with them, especially if, as in most situations, it is your mother who wants to run the wedding. There are six goals to this conversation:

☐ to state calmly and rationally your needs and desires

☐ to listen not only to what is being said to you but, just as important, to the anxiety, fear and pain lying underneath the surface of the words

☐ to offer reassurance, comfort, empathy and compassion

☐ to express your love and respect

☐ to attempt to reach a consensus by being open and flexible wherever you can

☐ to elicit their help, wisdom and support

There is much more at stake here than getting what you want for your wedding. By having an open, honest, loving discussion with your family you are, in fact, renegotiating your relationship from that of needy child to self-actualized woman. You are attempting to move from a state of dependency to an ideal state of interdependence. If the goal is for them to treat you as a mature woman with reasonable wants and needs, the last thing you want to do is throw adolescent tantrums, make unreasonable demands or dissolve in a puddle of tears.

It may be that you will not bring them over to your side the first time you discuss the wedding, or even the tenth time—you may even need outside help to resolve a major conflict—but you will gain more by being kind, respectful and accommodating wherever possible than you will by drawing the lines of battle.

If you are angry, hostile and demanding, flatly refuse their suggestions and offers of help or exclude them from the planning process, you unwittingly underscore their very real fear and sadness that they are losing you—which in turn makes them become all the more demanding and controlling! But if you hear and respond to the pain or fear that lurks behind their demands or actions and respond lovingly to it, you may well see a very real and immediate shift in attitude.

Sharing your wedding with your family can make warm, wonderful memories to be treasured for a lifetime. But in order for that to happen, you have to bring the gears of the Wedding Machine to a grinding halt. Forget about being a star. Forget about perfection and be yourself, the person they love. Your soul is not fed with designer cakes and country-club canapés but with the love and support of those dearest to you. When you are not chasing after impossible dreams of perfection, you can begin to share your desires and allow those you love to have a role in helping you create a wonderful wedding.

So before you lash out, *stop, think* and *listen*. You may find that you and your parents are not so far apart after all. One bride shared a wonderful story that illuminates this truth. As Traci tells it, the second she brought the first bridal magazine into the house her mother was "on it like a cat on a chipmunk." Every time Traci expressed a preference, her mother didn't like it.

"It made me crazy," Traci recalled. "We started fighting about everything. I felt like she was trying to run my wedding, and she kept insisting she wasn't. Fortunately I had to go back to college to finish my senior year, so we were apart from August until Thanksgiving. Distance gave me the perspective I needed to realize that I was blaming her for treating me like a child when I was the one doing it to myself. I had an infantile need for her to approve of my choices! She never said I couldn't or shouldn't buy a particular dress. She just said it wasn't her taste. After I saw that, I was a lot less defensive and we've gotten along fine."

Whither Thou Goest . . .

Sometimes, though, even when you do everything right there comes a point when you must face the issue of divided loyalties. Your fiancé or his family are adamant about some particular aspect of the wedding, and your family is equally adamant that it be handled their way. If you sense danger here, trust your instincts. Unless you confront it head-on right now, what should have been a simple disagreement stands a very good chance of setting a hazardous pattern that has the potential to reverberate throughout your marriage. Couples who fail to develop a sense of autonomy early in their married life soon find themselves in a continuous state of conflict.

One of the most oft-quoted lines of the Bible is "Therefore a man leaves his father and his mother and cleaves to his wife, and they become one flesh" (Genesis 2:24 RSV). Never is there a time more appropriate to discuss what this means than at this critical juncture in your relationship. If your pastor or counselor does not bring it up, you would be well advised to do so yourselves, not only if you have reached an impasse over an issue that has caused you to be on the opposite side of the fence from your parents but most especially if it is apparent that your parents have no intention of giving up control even after you are married.

Remember, there are supposed to be only two people in your marriage—you and your spouse. You cannot possibly "cling only unto thee" when you are running back and forth playing intermediary between your respective parents and each other.

However, the fact that the Bible, your pastor, your hearts and a battalion of psychologists agree that it is essential for you and your fiancé to support each other and stand firmly side by side at all times does not mean that you have license to gang up on whoever gets in your way. Two people assuming the role of enfant terrible are merely twice as unattractive as one person doing it. Asserting your solidarity, like most privileges, comes with its own set of responsibilities, the most important of which are the need to

☐ act with love and respect for all persons involved

☐ save declarations for big issues

☐ attempt at all times to reach an amicable solution

☐ refrain from making unkind remarks about each other's relatives to each other or to anyone else

You are, after all, setting the course for your adult life. The best way to forge an autonomous relationship is to act like a grownup, not like a rebellious child.

A perfect example of this in action was displayed when Tom and Margot ran headlong into a parental battle over alcohol at their wedding reception. Margot's family wanted an open bar, and Tom's made it clear that they did not want alcohol served at all. Margot herself wanted only peace, but Tom tended to side with his parents. For a while it was a touchy issue, and Tom and Margot found themselves arguing over it repeatedly.

"The more Tom would side with his parents, the more I wanted to side with mine, even though I really didn't care one way or the other!" Margot laughed. "Finally one night we looked at each other and said, 'This is crazy. We've got to settle this once and for all. And we need to work it out ourselves.' So that's what we did."

After talking it over, they decided that they did not need alcohol to have a good time and that they did not really want to set up a situation where it could be easily misused. So they would put one bottle of champagne on each table for toasting purposes, along with several bottles of sparkling grape juice. Their guests could select which beverage they wanted, but no one would have access to large amounts of champagne. Once this was decided, they went to both sets of parents and told them of their decision. Fortunately all four were so impressed by the reasonableness of the compromise itself plus the maturity it took to reach it that they were willing to leave it at that.

By taking the reins, displaying rational, loving solidarity and handling adult problems like adults, Tom and Margot set a strong, positive course for the future. They have established clearly where their loyalties lie, worked together to creatively solve a sticky problem by taking everyone's feelings into consideration, and made an essentially unpopular decision without alienating the people they love. Pretty impressive feat, wouldn't you agree?

The Lady Who's Left Out

No discussion of family would be complete without focusing on one very important but often overlooked person. Of all the relatives whom you may unintentionally hurt while making your wedding plans, the one most likely to feel like a second-class citizen is your future mother-in-law. Because she is the mother of the groom and therefore not traditionally a major player in the wedding drama, you can easily, and very often unintentionally, leave her out of the fun and planning. This is sad because it represents the loss of a viable opportunity for the two of you to get to know each other and begin developing a sense of "family." Also from a purely practical point of view, excluding her is a sure way to create problems that might have been avoided. If her feelings get hurt, if she feels discounted and underappreciated, she may act on those emotions by lashing out or becoming intractable over some triviality. She might even harbor a deep resentment that can mar your future relationship with her.

Many brides say they already have a mom and don't need another one. Perhaps that is true and you share the sentiment, but your mother-in-law very likely has no interest in undermining your relationship with your own mother. Not only is it safe to let her be close to you, but you may find that she has the potential to become a terrific friend and ally. Remember also that the two of you have one very important thing in common—you both love the same guy. In fact, were it not for her, that guy wouldn't even be here! How lovely it is when that shared love is allowed to take precedence and help you overcome your natural differences. If you let her be "one of the girls" as you exclaim over flowers and consider the merits of dresses and menus, she may prove to be a lot of fun, as well as a wealth of practical and creative knowledge.

A perfect example is the case of Moira and Brian, who will be married in three months. Because Moira chose to marry in Ohio, where she grew up, and her mother-in-law, Mary, lives in Michigan, distance proved to be a problem. Moira could not very well ask Mary to make a three-hour trip every time some detail of the wedding presented itself. So she thought about Mary's talents and interests and realized immediately that she was the only logical choice to accompany her to the florist. Her own mother doesn't know a daisy from an aster and freely admits it, whereas Mary has a marked talent for decorating and design and knows how to create elegance and beauty, especially with flowers. Mary was delighted to help and immediately agreed to come to Ohio and help sort out the daisies from the asters. Though she and Moira have very different tastes, they wound up with a plan that incorporated both of their favorites.

Remember that your mother-in-law feels keenly the same painful underlying sense of loss your own mother feels. As in dealing with your own family, it helps to be sensitive to the hidden hurts and vulnerabilities and not be so married to the idea of perfection that you have to do everything by yourself and in your own way. Ask her advice, show her your choices, keep her up to date on what is happening, and be sure to thank her for her help, advice and support. It may seem like a small thing, but she will appreciate your sensitivity and, in turn, appreciate you.

Expectations

A final word of caution: even the most simply beautiful wedding can get messy and complicated when it comes to family. You cannot dictate how people will behave. You cannot control how they feel, how they respond or how they fail to respond. If you aim to be kind, loving and inclusive, the most important thing you can do is to discard the notion of "the perfect family" at exactly the same moment you discard the notion of "the perfect wedding." People are not perfect. Even when they love you with all their hearts, they sometimes do and say hurtful things.

Too many brides make the mistake of expecting their families to turn into the Cleavers the minute the wedding date is circled on the family calendar. Much as you might like to have Ward and June smiling benignly around the dinner table, the fact is, the family you had before you got engaged is the exact same family you have today. Mom is not going to magically stop pestering you about your appearance, just as Dad is not going to suddenly hand over his credit card when he has spent his entire adult life being—uh—thrifty. Your sister is not going to stop borrowing your stuff without asking, and your brother most likely is going to continue to embarrass you in front of your friends.

The best thing you can do is try to anticipate problems and avoid them. If you know that Grandma gets querulous with cousin Ruth, then don't seat them at the same table. Likewise, if you know your sister feels threatened whenever she is told she "has" to do something, don't approach her like an army drill sergeant. Let her feel that she has some sense of autonomy, even if it is over something as minor as choosing her own hairstyle. The key is to be sensitive—something you cannot be as long as you cast yourself in the role of the Princess Bride.

When the photographer says, "Smile, everybody!" you want those smiles to be genuine. If you make your wedding a "family affair" they will. And your wedding album will be simply beautiful as a result.

8

All Good Gifts

I*n days gone by it was the custom to exhibit wedding gifts at the* home of the bride's parents. Guests would arrange to have their selections elegantly wrapped and shipped from local department stores days, or even weeks, before the wedding. Upon their arrival, the bride would promptly open the presents and place them on display in the dining room with their accompanying gift cards so visitors could walk amongst the splendor exclaiming over the silver teaspoons from Aunt Minnie and Uncle Beau in Savannah and the crystal salad bowl from the Johnsons down the street. If you're a fan of old movies, you know all about this. If you are not, it seems a risk to even mention it for fear someone might get the bright idea to revive it! Letitia Bainbridge, social secretary to the White House during the Kennedy administration, once said flatly, "Brides consider weddings loot time."

To be fair, elderly women who recall from past experience the custom of displaying wedding gifts, insist that it was a charming and innocent practice—which indeed it may have been given the less mercenary flavor of the times. But human nature being what it is, one still has to believe that at least occasionally pride, greed and oneupmanship reared their ugly heads. People just tended to be more discreet about it in those days.

A case in point is an essay entitled "Wedding Presents," in which Charles W. Morton, having received an invitation to the wedding of a couple he barely knew, writes, "The householder has been tapped, elected. He is an Old Friend—that is, a donor. Not to respond, he is made to feel, would throw the bride into hysterics, delay the rites, blight the romance, and even lend a twinge of scandal to the whole project."

Today, except for the presents given at prewedding showers, most wedding-related gifts are opened and viewed privately, or with close friends and family at a newly minted event called an "afterglow," customarily held the morning after the wedding. The bride and groom, their parents, close relatives and perhaps some members of the bridal party gather for brunch and a ritual unwrapping of the gifts. Typically this event goes one of two ways—either it turns out to be a wonderfully intimate respite after all the public hoopla of the days before, or it is akin to laying out the merchandise like goatskins at a Turkish bazaar. It all depends on the couple's attitude about gifts and gift-giving.

Waving the Magic Wand

As you have already seen, in an age of blatant consumerism who you are too often depends on what you own. No single entity understands this more clearly than the Wedding Machine, which has moved in for the kill like a hunter on the first day of deer season. Slick, glossy ads for fine china, flatware and crystal, most of which won't find its way onto the average newlyweds' dining table for at least a decade, if at all, are but a small part of it. Stores hold bridal seminars where couples not only learn how to choose items for their home but have their names entered in on-the-spot drawings, receive gift bags full of goodies and sometimes get the hard sell to register for the necessary accouterments. Some go much further. One bride related the story of going to a specialty shop to pick up the gifts her fiancé had ordered for his groomsmen.

"Would you like to enter our contest?" the salesman asked. "You could win a free wedding."

Dubious, the couple listened to the pitch. Turns out that the "free" wedding was a public spectacle inside the store where casual mall shoppers could see the festivities, drop in and hopefully do a little ordering of their own. Wisely, they declined.

Before the howls of protest begin, it must be stressed that there is nothing intrinsically wrong with registering for gifts. Ninety percent of today's brides and grooms do so, and many guests appreciate the convenience and sense of security they get from making a selection from a limited preapproved list of needed and wanted items. They don't have to worry about being the bearer of the fifth toaster or the fourth blender, are spared making difficult decisions regarding style, size and color, and are (presumably—but more on that later) certain they are giving you something you actually like and will use in your new home. However, the bridal registry practices of today are a far cry from what was intended when the first one opened sometime between World Wars 1 and 2.

The history of the bridal registry is actually rather difficult to nail down. Some sources credit a jewelry store in Milwaukee, Wisconsin, with coming up with the idea in 1917 since, in addition to engagement rings and wedding bands, jewelers also sold sterling flatware, trays, candlesticks and the like. Others claim department stores were the first to jump on the bridal bandwagon, while others credit a store called China Hall in Rochester, Minnesota, with hatching the first registry in 1901. But whoever took the gift by the ribbons, one thing is for certain—the bridal registry was simply a more formalized version of an already established practice. During the early 1900s, hometown news-papers routinely printed a list of items the engaged couple needed to set up housekeeping.

The goal of both the newspaper lists and the early registries was to inspire ideas and avoid duplications, both perfectly reasonable aims. However, two factors turned a practical idea into a problem: consumers and retailers colluding to create a society-sanctioned greedfest and technology providing the means to easily collect data and make it instantly available nationwide via computer. Aunt Margaret in Omaha now needs only to go to her local chain store and click a few keys to find out what brand of coffeemaker is wanted by her niece in Poughkeepsie. Many retailers no longer even have a consultant to help you make your selections at the bridal registry. Instead they hand you an object which they call a "scanning gun" but which in fact is a sort of magic wand that can be waved over the bar code on anything from pots and pans to CDs and clothes for your trousseau. To hold that wand, couples say, is to know the meaning of power.

"I'm ashamed to admit it, but we went crazy," one bride confessed. "We registered for anything and everything that caught our eye. The really embarrassing part is we actually got some of this stuff and couldn't even remember picking it out."

The bearers of the magic wand are also actively encouraged to ask for nontraditional gifts, a practice that benefits retailers who had been previously left out of the bridal registry loop. Today's couples register at art galleries, building supply stores, mail-order companies—you name it. The Federal Housing Administration has even thrown its hat into the matrimonial ring by making it possible for banks to set up funds where guests can deposit contributions toward a down payment on a house.

In and of themselves none of these things are necessarily wrong. In the case of second marriages, or where the bride and groom have been single long enough to have accumulated significant household goods, a nontraditional approach might actually be a breath of fresh air to frazzled gift-givers. The problem arises from how all this is handled. Too often couples register in multiple places, each one of which is only too happy to provide them with a card that can be mailed to potential gift-givers to alert them where to buy the goodies.

Before you go out to register, be aware that although it may be accepted practice to send such cards, the truly appreciative couple would not dream of doing anything so crass. Gifts are a voluntary token of love, not something expected and orchestrated. Certainly if someone wishes to know where you are registered it is permissible to tell them, but it is neither kind nor polite to even hint at what is desired.

Many brides who would never dream of soliciting gifts from friends and family inadvertently get swept up in the practice for the simple reason that it is presented to them at the registry as matter-of-factly as the price of breadmakers and espresso machines. Some bridal registries even prioritize your items. That is, rather than allow your guests to select at random, it lists things in the order of how badly you want them, which means that Aunt Mary could easily feel pressured into buying a forty-five-dollar goblet to complete your set when she would have been more comfortable with the thirty-dollar coffeemaker.

When you hear your friends talking about what they want, what they may get and how they intend to make sure they actually do, it is all too easy to get caught up in society's shamelessness regarding wedding gifts. One couple gleefully announced that they had found a way to beat the system by registering at a store that honored cash returns. Because many guests are averse to giving monetary presents, preferring a gift of more lasting and personal value, this pair registered for expensive china, crystal and flatware knowing full well they had no intention of keeping it. Sure enough, after the wedding they hauled it all back to the store, and without the slightest twinge of guilt, collected the cash. Since they were using this money toward a down payment on a home, the end, they felt, justified the sneaky means. The fact that they had deceived their guests and ripped off the store by costing them numerous employee hours and lost sales never entered their minds. They felt entitled to get what they wanted—and what they wanted was the green stuff.

As with the "perfect" twenty-thousand-dollar wedding, our society has developed the deeply entrenched attitude that brides and grooms have a right to expect a decent haul to offset the tremendous cost of hosting a reception. One newspaper, in an article about bridal registries, actually ran a headline that read "Picking Out Gifts That Count"—as opposed, one can only surmise, to gifts that *don't* count. Very likely no one in the newsroom even noticed a problem with it. That is how skewed our thinking has become about gifts in general, and about wedding presents in particular.

Come Bearing Gifts

One bride and groom candidly pointed out that since the lowest price they could obtain for the reception was twenty-five dollars per meal, they had to "seriously consider" who they could "afford to invite." Those who were judged as unlikely candidates in the good gift department got scratched off the list. Another woman says that not long after she received a wedding invitation she heard how the bride and groom had chosen to formulate their guest list. Because they wanted to be assured of receiving lots of presents, they had drawn up two lists, an A list and a B list. The A list got the first round of invitations. Anyone who sent back regrets was then promptly replaced by someone from the B list! Since she wasn't entirely sure whether she was an A or a B, the woman telling the story decided to make it simple and forgo the whole affair.

Other would-be wedding guests say that very often they go to the registry in hopes of selecting something they know is wanted, only to find that the couple has registered for nothing in a price range that even remotely matches their budget. "Sometimes the cheapest thing is a hundred dollars," one said, aghast. "Who can afford that?"

Too often, caught up in the heady whirl of stardom, couples fail to take into account anything beyond their own desires. Consequently they draft an unspoken agreement between hosts and guests that says, "I will spend X number of dollars to entertain you, and you will return the favor by bringing a gift that costs at least as much." According to a major credit card company, the average cost of a wedding gift these days is sixty-eight dollars. However, a recently published wedding guide calls a hundred dollars per gift "a nominal amount."

In addition to buying a costly gift for the wedding itself, guests such as bridesmaids, close friends and extended family feel burdened to bring gifts to the shower and sometimes even to multiple showers. One bride mentioned that between friends, family and future in-laws, she was scheduled to have ten! Not too many women have that many, fortunately, but many brides will have two or three, which means that the cost of gift giving can easily surpass the cost of hosting one couple at the reception.

Brides whose friends don't spontaneously throw them a shower also feel cheated and very often arrange to have one thrown, even if it means prevailing upon family members, pouting, having hysterics or acting like a martyr until someone relents and does the honors. Brides also admit that they freely offer their opinions as to what type it should be, what type of food should be served and where it should be held. One young woman stressed that she preferred an "around-the-clock" shower because "that way you can better control what you get." At an around-the-clock shower guests are assigned a time of day and are asked to bring something the couple might use at that particular hour—for example, a coffeemaker for 7:00 a.m. and a casserole dish for 6:00 p.m.

Legend has it that the first shower occurred due to dire circumstances. A young Dutch bride's father refused to give her a dowry because she had chosen to marry a penniless miller. Undeterred, she married the man she loved despite the fact that they had not even the barest necessities to set up a household. Seeing the situation and feeling pity for the pair, the groom's friends got together, pitched in what money and items they had, and "showered" the newlyweds with gifts they desperately needed.

Today need has very little to do with it—showers are an expected part of wedding festivities. Of course they are fun, and it would be lovely if every bride could have one, but it is not the bride's place to get one together, nor is it fair to expect costly gifts from bridesmaids and family members who already have a high financial stake in the wedding.

But as shameless as today's attitudes about gifts may seem, it pales in comparison to the latest reception practices. While many couples admit that they count on any extra gifts they can squeeze out of their guests to pay for the pricey honeymoon cruise they booked six months previously, only a few have the temerity to call the extraction of these monetary contributions "fun."

In some ethnic cultures it has long been the custom for brides to receive money in exchange for dancing with guests—as in the dollar dance. In some European cultures, for example, the bride puts on an apron with pockets to collect the cash. As long as everyone present is in agreement that this is a customary and acceptable part of the evening's entertainment, there is nothing wrong with it. Where it becomes a problem is when it is foisted on unsuspecting receptiongoers who feel they have already contributed to the newlyweds' future.

Believe it or not, these days couples blatantly pass beautifully decorated baskets to collect donations, or brides wear satin money bags that can be ordered commercially from bridal catalogs. In some cases brides even devise cute little games to make such emotional blackmail seem more palatable—perhaps to themselves. One such game came replete with an elaborate homemade game board. Guests who landed on, say, "romantic dinner for two" were required to fork over the cost of two meals at a restaurant with the proper number of stars after its name. If that sounds shocking and perhaps even unfathomable, then consider this: according to the *Wall Street Journal*, a Chicago inventor has patented a system "for streamlining gift commitments." This "system" consists of an electronic device that can be passed out to guests at the reception so they can enter into it their credit card numbers and the amount they wish to give.

"The impulse for a contributor, or gift giver, to make a pledge is maximized at the time a pledge is solicited," the patent papers say. "However, this impulse dissipates over time." In other words, catch 'em while they're (a) caught up in the romance of the moment or (b) too embarrassed to look like a tightwad in front of the other guests at their table.

Thank You Very Much . . .

Of course once all the goodies have been garnered, even if by questionable means, it only stands to reason that the happy couple would be eager to thank their benefactors. Very often, though, the expression of gratitude is discounted almost as much as the need for kindness and civility. Some brides and grooms try to squeak by with a blanket thank-you printed on their wedding favors or programs. Others take months to write a cursory note that makes no mention of what was given and is no more personal than a printed card. A few never seem to "get around" to sending notes at all.

"I meant to, but we were so busy getting settled, and then a bunch of time went by, and, well, I don't know . . ." one newlywed admitted, her voice trailing off. She shrugged, then giggled as though it were somehow cute to have made such a social and moral gaffe.

Perhaps when you were a child you were blessed with a mother who had an iron-clad rule—no gifts may be worn, read or played with until the proper thank-you card has been written. If so you were very lucky, because you understand in the marrow of your bones the importance of showing your appreciation for everything you have been given, including those things you do not especially like. No one says you have to love the purple satin sheets or the cream pitcher that looks like a cow. No one says you have to use them daily for the next twenty years.

True gratitude transcends differences in taste, colors that don't match and even ceramic cows that look like grinning Holsteins to reach a higher place—a place where you are simply thankful that the people you care about cared enough about you to have given you their time, good wishes and gifts. True gratitude smiles at the purple sheets, shakes its head fondly and says, "That's Aunt Mary for you. She sure loves the exotic." True gratitude tucks the ceramic cow in the cupboard and laughs with joy at the memory of the young cousins who washed the neighborhood dogs to buy it.

Another thought to contemplate as you think about your wedding gifts are gifts for which you cannot register. These are the handmade gifts, the heirlooms that are passed on and the gifts that are services rather than things which can be unwrapped. For example, your uncle, an amateur videographer, gives you a tape of your wedding and the highlights of the reception. Your elderly great-aunt presents you with a single English bone china teacup and saucer from her collection to start you on a collection of your own. Your brother, the budding potter, makes a handmade casserole dish with an ill-fitting cover. Too often these gifts can be overlooked either because their monetary value may not be obvious or because their "quality" doesn't match up to the conventional standard of perfection. But when someone gives you something they either made or cherish, they give twice—once with the item or service itself and the second time with a part of themselves. Never mind if it isn't "perfect." The imagination and joy that go into the creation of a gift given in love have transformative powers. But first you must look with new eyes and an open heart.

One bride proudly displays in her kitchen a painting of a covered bridge. On first glance it is rather impressive, but a closer look reveals that the proportion of trees to bridge is off by an artist's mile. The light is wonderful, though, and the snow so real you feel as though you could reach through the canvas and grab a handful. It was painted by her nephew, a high-school senior who displays remarkable, but still very raw, talent. The bride has no illusions about its being great art, but she likes to say that it was painted by a great artist.

There is yet another gift you get from each and every guest who attends your wedding that you might want to consider for its lasting value. Not many brides and grooms think about this, but the simple acceptance of a wedding invitation is a gift in itself. The act of sending back the card accepting your invitation is assurance that you mean enough to your guests that they will make whatever sacrifices are required to be present to share your day. Very often this means traveling a long distance, hiring babysitters, feeling uncomfortable because they don't know anyone and then having to bring a present on top of it all! In many cases families go to considerable time and expense—not to mention juggling schedules—to show up and share in your festivities. When you see yourself as the star they come to pay homage to, it is all too easy to lose sight of this fact.

One of the most beautiful songs in the Broadway musical *Godspell* is "All Good Gifts." It reminds us to thank the Lord, the source of "every good endowment and every perfect gift" (James 1:17), for the gifts he brings to us. What a lovely thought to contemplate in a world gone mad with greed! Whether or not you have a shower, get all twelve place settings of Lenox china or rake in enough cash to travel first class to the Cayman Islands is truly immaterial to the beauty and holiness of your wedding day. In three years' time most of the gifts you unwrapped will have been used up, replaced, given away or sold at a garage sale anyway. Even the cash will have been spent and forgotten.

What will remain in your heart always are the intangibles—the memory of your grandmother making the long flight from Florida to be with you despite her failing health, the laughter and fun provided by a friend who had no money to bring anything more than a single pillar candle that smelled of lavender, the advice and warm wishes written on the back of a card from your favorite professor. All these things and more are *good* gifts. Gather them up like rare and beautiful seashells to remind you forever of the mystery and magnificence of God's love channeled through the people in your life. As you write your thank-you notes, think about each person and how they enrich your life and tell them exactly that.

"But we have 350 guests invited!" one bride wailed when this idea was suggested to her. "How can I be expected to write something personal to each one?"

Three hundred and fifty notes is certainly mind-boggling, but the appreciative couple who truly treasures each and every guest will make the time to do it. If a guest is important enough to invite, is she or he not important enough to be remembered in a special way? Guests may not even realize it until they get one, but it is a delightful surprise to receive a card that goes beyond the cursory "Thank you for the vase. It looks lovely in our home," or the even more cursory "Thank you for your gift. We appreciate it." A message from the heart that says not only do we appreciate the vase but we appreciate *you* is the kind of card a simply beautiful bride sends with gratitude and joy.

A few couples who are already blessed with all the material things they need to set up housekeeping take gratitude to an even higher plane. Profoundly thankful for the gift of each other—and what a gift it is to have someone by your side to love, support, respect and honor you all the days of your life!—they look outside themselves and their own concerns. Instead of registering for another set of towels they don't need or leaving guests to their own creative devices, they suggest that gifts be given to their favorite charity in their name.

Not long ago a couple in their thirties, both of whom had fully equipped homes of their own, put a different spin on this idea by asking would-be gift-givers to donate to the charity of their own choice. After the wedding they found themselves supporters of education, the arts, a homeless shelter, a church food pantry, the local battered women's shelter and an agency that helps abused children, among many other wonderful things, some of which proved quite unusual. Much to their great delight, they even became the "adoptive parents" of a rhesus monkey at the zoo!

"Isn't this fantastic?" the bride asked, displaying her unusual gifts.

"You will laugh when I say this, but it's like Josh and I are a Roman candle that exploded and sent sparks everywhere into all these wonderful, giving places. It's really an awesome thing to realize that your love can make the world a better place."

What a wise statement, even when taken just at face value. Imagine what would happen if you were to extend that thought beyond the wedding and its gifts into all the years of your life together. When love is viewed as a gift in itself, you feel rich every day you are on earth. Sure, you might still wish you could buy decent furniture or get a CD player, but you don't let these wants destroy your life, your marriage or your peace of mind. Instead you give thanks for what you have and look for ways to multiply the blessings by sharing them with those who most desperately need your light and love.

Couples who begin their married life with a list of wants, or even worse, a list of "must haves" that stretch from here to the mall, set themselves up for a lifetime of dissatisfaction. No mater what they get or what they achieve, it is never enough. They are on to the next thing before the first one can even be savored. To be grateful in the moment, to know what it means to be thankful for even small things, is to give yourselves a gift that keeps on giving.

There is a lovely, poignant scene in the film *How to Make an American Quilt*. Throughout the movie a group of older women gather around a quilting frame to make a wedding quilt for the granddaughter of one of them, whom they have all known since she was a child. As they sew, they remember the past and retell incidents that brought them love, joy, pain, anger and even a sense of betrayal. They laugh, they argue, they cry, but through it all they stitch pieces of themselves with sturdy cotton thread into a lasting treasure for the young woman who stands on the threshold of a new life.

The most transcendent scene occurs at the very end of the movie, when the bride-to-be runs down the road toward the man she loves wrapped in her wedding quilt. In that exquisite early-morning moment it is not a mere blanket that enfolds her but the love of the women who shaped and guided her and gave her pieces of themselves made from whole cloth.

We don't make too many hand-stitched quilts in our speeded-up world, but well-chosen gifts, including those of little or no monetary value, are everywhere, showering down upon you throughout your wedding season like gentle rain if only you open your eyes and heart to see them. Don't concentrate only on what comes in an envelope or a box bearing a beautiful bow. Look instead to what is inside the hearts and eyes of the people you love, for it is there that you will find the most beautiful gifts of all.

9

Let 'Em Eat Cake

I *consider my wedding a workday,"* the bride-to-be commented. A small silence fell as five people stared at her. Four were clearly aghast, one merely quizzical.

"Huh?" the latter asked. "I don't get it. I thought your wedding was supposed to be fun."

"It is," she replied breezily. "But since my fiancé and I are hosting it, we don't feel we can afford to just cruise. We have a responsibility to our guests. We think of it as a dinner party, only bigger."

Silence again as the other young women in the group assimilated this clearly foreign information.

"Well, I certainly don't see it that way," one of the shocked ones said, once she'd recovered. "To me, that's what you hire catering people for. As far as I'm concerned, my wedding is my day and I don't have to do a darn thing except show up and look great."

It may sound crass when stated so boldly, but the fact is, most brides and grooms agree, at least secretly. The idea of the star, or stars, of the production having any personal responsibility for the well-being of the "audience" seems vaguely alien. After all, whoever heard of the leading lady worrying about whether the seats in the balcony are comfortable or whether there is enough popcorn at the concession stand? The star's concerns are strictly personal—how she looks, how she feels, both physically and emotionally, at any given moment, and how people are responding to her and her sumptuous backdrop.

To some extent some of these thoughts are even legitimate, especially shortly before and during the wedding itself. Brides and grooms need and deserve a few reflective moments to be unconcerned about anything other than what they are about to do when they meet at the altar. Once there, they are entitled to the freedom to focus on each other and the vows they are exchanging without worrying whether anyone remembered to chill the sparkling grape juice. But the issue here is not a few moments of personal time—it is the attitude that the wedding is for the couple only and that the guests, the clergy and the service providers are merely "extras" included to provide or admire the decor and bring the festive scene to life.

This is one area where the Wedding Machine cannot be blamed for the infractions committed by couples who choose to be self-centered. Many rainforests have been felled in the creation of lavish wedding books and slick magazines stressing the importance of etiquette, lovely surroundings and delicious food to delight the senses and increase the enjoyment of the day for those who come to share it. No author of wedding literature would encourage you to be inhospitable and ungracious, or even tacitly approve of self-indulgence at the expense of others. But it happens—and more often than you may realize.

There are two very good reasons for this. The first boomerangs right back to the strong cultural message our society sends to young women about what it means to be a bride. Given that your wedding is "the most important day of your life," it is not surprising that too many brides internalize this to mean that their responsibility stops the moment they attach the veil to their head, take a deep breath and head for the door of the church.

In the planning stage they may gladly take into account such things as handicap accessibility, the provision of paper fans for an August ceremony if the church is not air-conditioned, and the need for vegetarian entrées. But once the "Wedding March" begins, it is as though a flock of little Walt Disney bluebirds flies in, lifts all sense of account-ability from Cinderella's shoulders and carries it away like a wisp of chiffon. From that moment on, the onus is off the star and onto the hired help. The other part of the problem is that our culture too often confuses hospitality with orchestrating a knock-their-socks-off produc-tion. Any time aesthetics are paramount, people's feelings, comfort and special needs all take a back seat to the creation of a perfect setting against which to act out the drama. Nowhere is this more evident than in the way the typical bride plans her wedding.

It would seem that the logical first step in wedding planning would be to draw up a list of all the people with whom you want to share your day and then figure out what type of party you can afford to host for that many people. But that is not usually the way it is done. Most couples today freely admit that they first determined what amenities they wanted and then manipulated the guest list to accommodate it. In other words, if it got to be too expensive to host 250 at the country club, the list got trimmed. Never once was the virtue of hospitality even considered.

Virtue? It may seem startling to use the word *virtue* alongside the word *hospitality*. Generally, books about virtue are shelved in the religion and ethics section of the bookstore and those about hospi-tality in the lifestyle section. Between the two areas lies a vast canyon filled with topiary centerpieces and charming invitations fashioned from handmade paper. When we think of hospitality these days we think of Martha Stewart, not of the Bible. And yet in the pages of Scripture lies everything you ever needed to know about compas-sion, kindness, prudence and a sense of fair play—all the hallmarks of true hospitality.

Most brides do not mean to be inhospitable. They sincerely want the people they invite to have a wonderful time and take home a lovely memory. It's just that they get so caught up in the fulfillment of their own fantasies that they lose sight of what it takes to make that happen. As we have seen in previous chapters, a sense of entitlement, an obsession with perfection and a greed for gifts can cause couples to do incredibly tacky, ungracious and even outrageous things. Fortunately, the oversights most brides and grooms commit are usually small and are forgiven or overlooked by most guests. Yet many of these small gaffes can be avoided by the simple act of becoming attuned to the true meaning of hospitality.

The Care and Feeding of Guests

Hospitality begins right at the start, at the very moment you embrace the attitude that each and every single person who attends your wedding, however young or old, or however well you know them, is special. As a gracious host you have the job of acting in a manner that makes every guest feel your joy in their presence. Of course this doesn't mean that you have to serve the canapés yourselves, replenish the buffet table, wipe up spilled drinks or perform any of the other hosting jobs required when you throw a party in your own home. You mostly likely have paid staff or family volunteers to handle those things, and it is perfectly acceptable to let them do their job. Your job is to be generous and gracious without worrying about your "star quality" and how much attention you are receiving.

The savvy bride and groom realize that it isn't necessary to worry about being the stars anyway, because they know they automatically are the center of attention by virtue of their status as bride and groom. Everyone is there to see you. The least any hospitable couple can do is return the favor by being gracious. You will have plenty of time to be wrapped up in your own private world. That is what the honeymoon is for. Until the moment when you finally say goodbye and head for your hotel, you have an obligation to make sure the people who cared enough to be there feel welcome.

Very often the most unkind things couples do are a result of a subtle and almost subterranean feeling that there are two classes of guests— the "real" ones you were delighted to invite and everybody else. "Everybody else" includes the relatives you feel "stuck" with, the business associates you "have to" invite for "professional reasons" and the friends or significant others of your friends whom you don't know or don't especially like.

Very few brides are rude enough to actually tell a guest, "I am inviting you for professional reasons, but I can't afford to include your spouse, so I would appreciate it if you came alone"—though, believe it or not, it has been known to happen. More frequently second-class guests are invited with a blanket invitation.

One bride who worked for a large corporation posted an invitation on the bulletin board in her department along with a Post-It note saying, "Let me know whether or not you are coming! Bring your spouse or significant other, but no kids please." Other second-class guests are included on their friend's personal invitation as "and guest" or "and friend." When they arrive at the wedding, these are the guests who undergo the most severe scrutiny. Did they bring at least a token gift? Are they dressed appropriately? How are they behaving? Second-class guests sometimes can't win. On the one hand they are criticized for being too reticent and "standoffish" and on the other for having too much fun.

A rather outspoken bride expressed bitter displeasure that a girlfriend of one of her husband's friends, whom she had never met before that day, caught the bridal bouquet she had intended for her maid of honor. But another bride had the opposite view—she complained that a guest "just sat there all night like a bump on a log" and refused to take part in the tossing of the bouquet even though she was single and eligible! Being a tagalong can sometimes be very awkward indeed.

Second-class guests also tend to get abandoned. If they happen to be the primary but less eagerly anticipated invitee, they are sometimes not given the option of bringing along a friend to shelter them from the awkwardness of venturing forth alone into a world populated by couples. This is especially unkind when the single person knows few of the other guests. They also very often get seated toward the back of the room and after the first perfunctory greeting are ignored for the rest of the evening.

A charming bride and groom make every effort to seat these guests with people with whom they are most likely to be compatible. They also extend every effort to introduce them to people seated at other tables, personally invite them to participate in every activity and make sure their needs are met along with everyone else's. While it is only natural for the bride and groom to gravitate toward their own friends, especially once the festivities get into full swing, it is important not to be so cliquish that others feel as though they have been left out of the "in" club. Guests who feel ill at ease will very likely drift away early.

Another area where couples can fall short of graciousness is failing to consider the ages of their guests. Very likely these will be mixed. You will have everyone from elderly people to very small children or at least young adolescents. Admittedly this presents a challenge when it comes to menu choices and entertainment, but the gracious couple tries to vary the offerings so that there is something for everyone. Older guests do not enjoy a night of raucous rock music, just as younger guests would be less than enchanted with a night of waltzes. But a mix of music, like a mix of foods, adds to the fun and very often turns the party into an intergenerational celebration.

True hospitality also means being aware of any special needs specific guests may have and planning for them. One bride knew that an elderly guest, as a result of a permanent surgical procedure, can eat no solid food other than ice cream. Although ice cream was not on the menu, she arranged to have some brought in especially for him. It cost her very little to be thoughtful and made him feel as though he was not a burden but a welcome participant.

There are, however, some behaviors that get perpetrated on all guests, including the couple's closest friends and family members. One of the most common, and also the most annoying, is the long lag between the ceremony and the reception. Once the couple leave the church with their attendants, they often form a receiving line. On the surface that may seem like the gracious thing to do, but remember that the first people through the line are also the first to reach the reception, whether it is on or off site. It may be another half-hour or longer before the bride and groom finish greeting all their guests, especially if they have a great many. When the final guests head for the reception hall, the wedding party holds up production even longer by taking countless photos—which means that dinner is delayed and hapless guests are left to their own devices, most often at another location.

"I left a wedding once because of this," a guest asserted. "I am not kidding when I say that I sat for two hours waiting. Finally I thought *Who needs it?* and went home."

Other guests share these reception horror stories:

"I think the worst thing is when they have all this fancy-schmancy show-off food and nothing for kids to eat, even though they say kids are welcome."

"The worst is when they crank the music up so loud it deafens everybody over thirty. I remember a wedding once where it was so loud it was painful. I asked if they could turn it down just a little and the bride said, 'Our friends like it like this. If you don't like it, you can always leave.' That is exactly what I did."

"One of the most appalling things I've ever had to endure at a wedding was a slide show. I swear this is true—the bride's mother spliced all the slides she had taken of her daughter growing up with all the ones the groom's family had taken of him. We had to sit through forty-five minutes of home movies. I thought I would self-destruct before it ended."

"Once I went to a wedding where the food ran out before everybody had been through the buffet line and nobody seemed to notice. Finally someone pointed it out to the bride, who shrugged, waved her hand vaguely in the direction of the house—this was a garden reception— and went back to talking to her friends, all of whom had heaping plates."

"When my cousin got married, it was out of state and there were only about ten of us from Ohio. We didn't know anyone except each other and it stayed that way. You'd have thought we had leprosy or something. Everybody had this big old bash and we sat there looking like we'd crashed the party."

Every one of the above scenarios could have been avoided had the bride and groom been aware of their guests' feelings. Many thousands of dollars are spent on creating a stunning decor and serving a gourmet meal, yet being kind comes with no price tag at all. Could it be that that is why it is often so underrated? Horst Shulze, head of the supremely elegant Ritz-Carlton Hotel, put it best when he said, "Elegance without warmth is arrogance."

Do Me a Favor . . .

When ten brides were asked what one thing they could do to show their appreciation to their guests at the reception, six of them replied, "Give them a really great favor." Wedding favors—small gifts left at each place at the table for the reception—are an old custom that has currently come back into vogue in a rather big way. Generally favors are small, inexpensive items such as Jordan almonds gathered in tulle and tied with a ribbon, or bookmarks or seed packets commercially printed with the couple's name and the date. At high-end weddings the couple may elect to give miniature candy boxes filled with two gourmet chocolates or small silver-plated picture frames. Whether homemade or purchased, these token gifts are meant to be indications of the couple's gratitude as well as a souvenir of the occasion. In times past favors such as a silver ring, a thimble and a tiny wedding bell were baked into the cake and thought to bring good fortune to the lucky guests who found one.

Whether or not you choose to have wedding favors is strictly up to you—there is no "right" or "wrong." It all depends on what you can afford and how much the practice means to you. But as you make your decision, you might want to bear in mind what wedding favors can and cannot do. They can certainly look charming—at one wedding the couple gave paperback books of classic romantic novels tied up with ribbon and silk roses and fitted out with a pretty card that read, "Thank you for sharing our special day. May the stories of your life be filled with love." Favors can also be a momentary delight, especially if the gift is exceptionally unusual, pretty or unexpected. They can even have an enduring positive effect on the environment if you choose something natural like pine tree seedlings. What wedding favors cannot do, however, is make your guests feel truly honored and appreciated.

Unless your attitude is selfless graciousness from start to finish, a souvenir, however lovely, will not seem to be anything more than part of the "show." One bride, an artist, spent countless hours painting miniature pictures that were placed on tiny easels at each place setting. They were exquisite and artfully presented, but she admits that they had more to do with her enjoyment of the creative process and the outpouring of compliments they generated than with any real generosity. Unfortunately many favors get left on the table after the party, and even those that do make it home usually wind up in a junk drawer, never to see the light of day again until the couple being honored have children in college!

A favor is truly an act of kindness when it comes in the form of a gift bag for children filled with quiet, inexpensive toys to keep them occupied until dinner is served. Stickers, crayons, pads of paper, small puzzles and the like are appreciated by both parents and kids, and show families that you are glad they brought their little ones to share the day. Overall, favors can be expressions of the genuinely warm thoughts you hold in your heart for your guests, or they can be superfluous decorations. Your guests will know which by how welcome they feel.

A World of Our Own

Of course even the most well-meaning hosts can sometimes do hurtful things, not out of greed or mean-spiritedness but because they don't think or become too self-absorbed to notice anything outside their personal orbit. Unless the priest or minister is a close friend of the family, he or she is not invited for dinner. The disk jockey or band performs the entire evening, but no one fixes them a plate or gets them anything to drink. No one compliments the chef on the lovely buffet or thanks the waiters and waitresses for their hard work. It is as though the bride and groom and their party were caught inside a beautiful iridescent bubble and everybody outside of it not only doesn't count but doesn't even exist!

This is especially true when the bride and groom become too fixated on each other. It used to be that couples left their reception early, long before it was officially over. The bride tossed her bouquet, changed into her "going away" suit and was waved away by guests who then continued to celebrate for hours. Today the trend is for the bridal couple to stay until the last song is played or the last crumb of cake is polished off. While it can be wonderful to share in every exquisite moment of your special day, it does extend the hours of your commitment as hosts.

Like most brides and grooms, you will most likely feel totally swept away by the beauty, glamour and romance of it all. There is also a very palpable sense of relief that you finally accomplished the thing that has consumed so much of your time and so many of your thoughts for the past year or more. You want to shout, "Yay! We did it and it's great! Now we can let down!" Well—yes and no.

You certainly want to have fun—your enjoyment of the festivities absolutely increases the enjoyment of your guests. But you do need to be careful about being self-absorbed. Everyone is delighted to witness a few stolen kisses or a sweet exchange of glances, but no one wants to see the entire romance played out on the dance floor. Excessive displays of affection are neither appropriate nor kind, as they make guests feel like extraneous baggage and can also embarrass them. And while we're on the subject of embarrassment, it's wise to talk with your disk jockey or emcee, if you are having one, ahead of the festivities. As our society becomes looser about sexual innuendo, you can wind up inadvertently embarrassing not only your guests but yourselves as well!

Rules and Regs

Technically, your responsibility to be hospitable encompasses your behavior at any and all parties or festivities held in your honor, not just at the reception. But there is one other area that requires, if not hospitality exactly, a sense of graciousness. Too many ministers and service providers have shared too many horror stories for the subject to be ignored.

When you choose a site, both for your wedding and for your reception, there will be certain restrictions with which you must comply. Although most of these may be imposed by your church, even reception sites may have specific rules. Sometimes you are forbidden to bring in food or beverages from outside the restaurant or club that is catering your reception. Other times you are asked to keep the party confined to a specific area. These are serious obligations that you need to honor not only because there may be a monetary price to pay if you don't but also because you have a moral obligation to be respectful of the points spelled out in a contract.

Usually, though, most of the problems couples encounter regarding rules and regulations revolve around the printed guidelines sent by a church after interest is expressed in having the wedding there. Couples too often take the attitude that since it is their day, they should have the right to do whatever they want—write their own vows, select their own music, toss birdseed or rice with merry abandon and play "My Funny Valentine" at the benediction.

An Episcopal priest expressed his shock when the mother of the bride began rearranging the furniture around the altar the night of the rehearsal dinner. It seems she felt that the altar "was in the way." Another minister of a liturgical denomination was likewise astounded to hear that a couple wanted a country-western band to set up in the church and play a medley of oldtime gospel and pop tunes. Other clergy complained about videographers who stood in front of the pews and blocked the view of family members, photographers who ignored the no-flash request and endless receiving lines that kept them from being able to clean and prepare the church for Sunday services. One minister even shared the story of a family bringing take-out food into the church to munch on during the rehearsal.

These examples may seem extreme, but such things happen with enough regularity to require churches to explicitly spell out what is required of the wedding party and their guests. Sometimes even couples who are active members get so wrapped up in the specialness of their day that they forget that, first and foremost, a wedding is a solemn religious ceremony. In some Christian denominations it is also considered a sacrament. Every denomination regards it as a sacred rite that must be approached with respect and dignity from the prelude music all the way through to the recessional and postlude.

Though moments of mild levity are usually not inappropriate and can even be delightful, a wedding is not meant to be a scene of great hilarity. One wedding guest reported attending a wedding in a large church where the bride came down the aisle cracking jokes to the guests at the ends of the pews. Throughout the service the bride and groom continued the merriment by exchanging asides and laughing—even as they were reciting their vows!

Sometimes, however, you may feel that your church's rules are either unfair or without basis, a common enough complaint. This happened to a young bride who wanted to hire a string quartet but was told she could not due to the church's contract with the organist, who as one of his "perks" is granted the right to play for an additional fee at all weddings and funerals.

"It seems pretty arbitrary to me that I should have to have something I don't want," she said. "But the rules are the rules. If I want to be married there—and I do—then I have no choice but to abide by their decision. It's more important that I be married in my own church than it is to have special music. Sometimes you have to weigh your priorities."

Hopefully you are able to be as mature as the young woman in the above example. Most churches will work overtime to provide you with a beautiful ceremony, but it is your responsibility to cooperate and honor whatever idiosyncratic rules may be presented. Certainly you can politely inquire as to whether there is room for compromise on any rule that seems extreme, but if it becomes clear that there is no room for discussion, then the church has the final authority. If you decide the church is paramount in your plans, you have no real choice but to let go of the issue and concentrate on making your wedding as solemn, beautiful and free from negativity and anger as you possibly can. As the bridal couple, remember, you set the tone for the day.

The Sum of All Parts
Now that you have examined the various aspects of planning a wedding, hopefully you are eager to begin putting the "simply beautiful" principles to work. Even if you have already begun making plans and have locked in some choices you regret, it is not too late to change your mind about how you will handle the rest of your decisions. If you spent too much money in one area, you can always cut back in another and use your imagination to come up with something more creative than costly. If you have hurt someone, been neglectful of your fiancé or inconsiderate of your wedding party, family or friends, it is also not too late to make amends.

Change your mind. Change your heart. And begin right now to live with simple grace. What better place to start than at the beginning of a glorious new life?

And now . . .

Mary Claire Mutzabaugh

and Aaron Olson,

together with their parents,

Request the honor of your presence

at their

Simply Beautiful Wedding,

Saturday, July 19, 1997,

at two o'clock p.m.

at St. Joseph's Church,

Warren, Pennsylvania.

Reception to follow

at the Conewango Club

at five o'clock p.m.

10

Simply . . . Beautiful

Sunlight curled around the edges of the curtains in the upstairs bedroom of the brick Cape Cod house on Madison Avenue where Mary Claire Mutzabaugh grew up. Under the pink and lavender coverlet made five generations ago from wool shorn from the sheep raised by her grandmother's grandmother, she stirred, blinked and stared groggily at the familiar mint-green wallpaper. At first it seemed like an ordinary summer Saturday. The bedside clock read 7:30, which meant there was plenty of time to doze, shower, enjoy a leisurely breakfast and . . .

A sudden realization jolted her upright. It was July 19, 1997. She didn't need a calendar to confirm it either—the crazy timestep her heart was doing was proof enough.

"I'm getting married today!" she shouted at top volume.

Over their morning coffee at the breakfast table her parents, Helen and Paul, laughed at their daughter's exuberance. "Good morning!" they called up the stairs.

Every nerve danced with excitement, but Mary made no move to swing her legs over the side of the old twin-sized bed she'd had since junior-high days.

Soon enough she would join her mom and dad for hugs and kisses in the kitchen, but first she needed to read the letter waiting on the nightstand. Her fiancé, Aaron Olson, had given it to her the previous night after driving her home from their rehearsal dinner. She had written him a letter too, and they had agreed when they'd exchanged them not to sneak so much as a peak until morning. But the truth is, she had been too emotionally spent after the dinner to do anything but sit on the top step of her parents' staircase and cry.

All the months of planning and dreaming, the flurry of last-minute details, the exhaustion of wrapping up loose ends at the Medina County District Library where she works as a reference librarian and the long trip from her home in Medina, Ohio, to her parents' home in Warren, Pennsylvania, had poured out in one sudden, healing burst of tears. Though the uncharacteristic "waterworks" had upset her mother at first, Mary had assured her nothing was wrong.

"I'm just crying, that's all," she'd said helplessly. It wasn't much of an explanation, but Helen Mutzabaugh understood. It was plain that her daughter was temporarily overwhelmed by the enormity of what she was about to do.

To Mary's surprise Aaron, usually calm and controlled, had cried last night too. During the rehearsal when the priest had walked them through the wedding service, he had been overcome with emotion.

"Oh, that's so darling," Helen had murmured in the front pew.

But Mary knew exactly what he was feeling. She too experienced that sudden welling up inside. But for her the tears refused to come then. Instead she thought to herself, *So. It all comes down to this, this hour spent in God's house.*

Now she read the letter, smiled and folded the paper, thinking back over the history she had shared with this man who in just six and a half hours would become her husband. They had begun dating eight years previously, right here in Warren at the end of high school. Though they had parted for college with the agreement that they were both free to see other people, every summer and holiday had brought them back together as surely and swiftly as a pair of magnets. And then, two years ago, while she was still in graduate school, he had asked her to marry him. She looked down at the wide gold band of pave diamonds she wore as an engagement ring and chuckled, remembering.

"What Do You Think About Getting Married?"

Aaron Olson was not the kind of guy to propose with flowers, a romantic dinner and a diamond solitaire hidden in the baked alaska. Nor was he the sort to arrange for a lighted scoreboard to pop the question for him in front of three thousand screaming basketball fans. He would ask the woman he loved for her hand the way he did most things—casually. *Very* casually.

They had taken the ferry from Maumee, Ohio, to Put-In-Bay, a popular tourist mecca on Lake Erie's South Bass Island. The day was blue and gold—glorious—with a slight breeze blowing off the lake. A line of boats docked at the pier bobbed in the gentle waves, and the few cars allowed on the island during the summer wended their way carefully through streets thronged with tourists. After returning the tandem bike they had rented to take them cruising along the waterfront toward Perry's Monument, Mary and Aaron strolled down the sidewalk past a row of ice-cream stands, restaurants and shops selling anything capable of sporting a lighthouse design.

Suddenly he asked, "What do you think about getting married?"

"I think that would be fine," she replied in the same even tone. But her heart was turning cartwheels.

Oblivious to the hordes of people walking past them licking soft-serve ice-cream cones, Aaron stopped, reached into his pocket and pulled out a small brown velvet box. Mary's heart pounded crazily and her hands shook at she opened it. For a second she could only stare, her eyes as wide as two blue moons. She was temporarily at a loss for words.

"But, but . . ." she sputtered finally. "This isn't . . ." And then she laughed.

Nestled against the satin lining of the box lay a gold-colored ring sporting a green plastic stone and an adjustable band. Aaron's mom had won it in the arcade at Midway Park, an amusement center Mary and Aaron liked to frequent after dinner when they visited his parents on New York's Lake Chautauqua. His mother had put it in a jeweler's box to tide him over until there was time to get the real thing. Mary slipped it on her finger—and kept it there—until a Friday evening several weeks later when she visited him at his parents' home and found another jeweler's box on the bed in the guest room. That time, of course, her sputtering was for an entirely different reason. The wide band of pave diamonds was exactly what she had dreamed of.

Now she picked up the phone and dialed Aaron's number. Reminiscing was fun, but it was time to look ahead. At this perfect, blessed moment the future seemed as bright and shining as the path of a meteor, its destination as vast and unfathomable as the night sky. Yet she knew deep down that she was more than ready for wherever that path would take her. Hearing Aaron's voice on the other end of the line only confirmed it, as did the sure knowledge that they had put more work into planning their marriage than they had into making arrangements for the wedding.

Besides counseling intensively with the parish priest at St. Joseph's Catholic Church in Warren, they had taken the Prepare survey and attended a pre-Cana in Wellington, Ohio. The latter had been an intense day of listening to seasoned couples talk about the intricacies of a long-term relationship, of writing to each other and talking through their feelings, and of praying and giving thanks for the miracle of each other. The fact that it had culminated in a surprise Italian dinner served bistro style at a candlelit table for two was pure enchantment, like waking up to find a fairy ring on the front lawn. Unlike many couples who felt they "had" to be there, Mary and Aaron had given themselves up totally to the experience. For them, marriage meant the same lifetime commitment they had seen both sets of parents model. No escape hatches. No equivocating. And definitely no divorce.

Now they talked only a very a short while, because the bridesmaids were on their way over for breakfast. Downstairs, Paul Mutzabaugh was already busy decorating. Just so there would be no mistake as to which house was hosting the party, he attached a balloon bouquet to the porch railing and was preparing to head toward his beloved perennial garden to cut fresh flowers for the table. At eight-thirty Mary's three closest friends burst through the front door, full of bright chatter and excitement, to feast on Helen Mutzabaugh's special egg casserole, fresh fruit and muffins and watch Mary open her gifts from them. It was the last time she would hang out with "the girls" before the big event, and Mary loved every second of it, though she did sneak away once more to talk to Aaron: about 10:30 he called her to say that he was already getting dressed, even though the wedding wouldn't start until 2:00!

At 11:00 the bridesmaids left to start getting ready also, and once again Mary found herself alone in her room. "The Dress" hung from a hook on the back of the door, freshly pressed by the bridal salon and shrouded in heavy plastic. It was a simple creation—ivory, traditional, sleeveless, with a lace bodice but with no train or veil. This lack of veil had caused her mother some consternation in the beginning, but Mary assured her that a headband of fresh flowers was a better choice for her. "I look like a cupcake with frosting!" she'd exclaimed when she looked in the mirror and saw her small delicate face peering out of a cloud of tulle and lace.

As tiny and slender as she is, Mary wanted to steer clear of bouffant gowns with trains, bodices so heavily beaded they felt like plates of armor, and especially headpieces that resembled the wimple of the Flying Nun. For her gown, her wedding and her life, Mary's philosophy is "less is more." Besides, she preferred to come down the aisle wearing the dress, rather than have the dress, train and veil float down wearing *her*.

"You could attach a small veil to the headband," her mom had suggested, making one last-ditch stand for tradition.

But Mary had shaken her head no.

"I didn't say another word," Helen Mutzabaugh recalls. "I told myself, *You already had your wedding. This is hers.* It's hard sometimes to be the mother of the bride because you think your way is the right way. But I'm glad I stood back and let Mary do what she wanted."

Completely ready now with the headband of multicolored fresh flowers in place on her fluffy blond bobbed hair, Mary could hardly believe the transformation. Unlike most little girls growing up, she had never played wedding or walked her Barbie and Ken dolls through their matrimonial paces. Later, when her sorority sisters were planning what she calls "dreamboat weddings," she had felt curiously detached from all the hoopla, even though she ended up as a bridesmaid in four of them.

"I guess I just never imagined myself as queen for a day," she says with a shrug.

Perhaps that is because there is no history of big weddings in her family. Her parents had married rather late, especially given the times—her mom was twenty-six and her dad thirty-eight. For two adults firmly entrenched in their respective careers, a small church wedding with a dozen guests, dinner at a local restaurant, roses cut from the backyard and a cake made by the bride's mother seemed more appropriate than an ingénue affair with all the frills and furbelows. Her mom had worn a blue sheath dress that could be worn again and a simple lace mantilla. By that standard Mary knew that her own wedding was something of a production—even though she had worked overtime to keep it as simple as possible.

One Small Simple Problem

In the beginning her desire for simplicity had actually been a point of contention. Aaron's family, who were infinitely more social people than her own family, had expected a big event. They were in the throes of planning a large wedding for their daughter and had just assumed that their son would follow suit. Had it been left up to Aaron they probably would have too, but Mary had been appalled at the idea of breaking the bank for a single day. And so they had struck their first compromise—she agreeing to a bigger event than she would have planned left to her own devices, and he settling for a smaller one.

Mary's parents had given her seven thousand dollars—no strings attached—to spend on a wedding, furniture, the down payment on a house or any combination thereof. This amount had actually been another compromise. Her dad had been willing to offer more, her practical mom a bit less—which of course meant that they too had had to play a game of give-and-take. Mary budgeted carefully and was able to get everything she wanted for the wedding without spending a penny more—in fact, she actually came in *under* budget. All she lacked of the "usual" wedding accouterments were limos and a videographer, neither of which she cared a whit about, so she felt not the slightest sense of deprivation.

She and Aaron had also made their own invitations to save money. They had selected good-quality card stock from a stationer, had their message simply printed at a local print shop, and then decorated the front with a rubber-stamp design and embossing powder which Mary then hand colored. The compliments had flowed in almost as fast as the acceptances. Of the 104 carefully chosen people they had invited, 82 had sent back the enclosed postcard indicating that they would be there—about average, according to wedding consultants.

They had begun with two totally different philosophies about what constituted a wedding, but Mary and Aaron had worked out their differences remarkably well. The only real clash had come about a month after the invitations had been mailed, when a friend of a friend expressed displeasure through one of the groomsmen that she had not been invited. Neither Mary nor Aaron knew her well, but Aaron, hoping to avoid a potential problem, made a case for inviting her anyway. Mary, however, firmly defended the integrity of the list they had devised together.

"We had agreed from the beginning that it was important not to make our wedding be for other people," she asserted. "So whenever we were in doubt we always came back to that. It's not that we didn't care about other people's feelings. We did, very much, and we made a lot of decisions which reflected that. But we had agreed that it was up to us to make the final decisions, not other people, and most especially not people we didn't know."

They ended up not issuing an invitation. The conflict, they agreed, taught them an important lesson about the need to put their marriage first.

Get Me to the Church on Time

Mary looked at herself one last time in the mirror, this time holding her bouquet—a riot of pink, coral and blue summer flowers. The daughter of a serious gardener, she had taken special care at the florist's shop and had turned an unusual idea into something simple but stunning.

She and her bridesmaids had reached an easy decision on the attendants' dresses by steering clear of the bridal salon and searching in the Better Dresses department for something that could actually be worn again. Every single woman had had the experience of being told by a bride, "I'm picking something practical," only to find herself on the day of the wedding encased in neon-bright taffeta with puffed sleeves and a sash the size of a small Third World country. But Mary was true to her word. Together she and her bridesmaids selected simply cut street-length black dresses with coral, blue and pink flowers spilling like watercolors over the surface—perfect for solid-color bouquets for each bridesmaid. One would carry pink, another coral and the third blue, with the bride carrying her medley of all three.

Downstairs the news was that the photographer was late. Amazingly, Mary felt no sense of stress or tension—just a tingling of excitement that felt like tiny bursts of electrical current zipping up and down her spine. If something went wrong she would deal with it. The important thing was to not let anything spoil the wonder of this day.

Already there had been a tiny mishap, and she had handled that very well. Yesterday they had not been able to reach the cake baker, with whom they had had no contact since placing their order. Despite a small barrage of messages, she did not call back. For a moment Mary had panicked—what would happen if there was a mix-up and the baker had not filled their order? But then, almost immediately, she had thought, *Then we won't have cake. And it will be all right.* In the end though, the baker had called back and all was well in the dessert department. The cake table would be graced with a small three-tiered white confection with raspberry filling, ivory buttercream frosting in a basketweave pattern and a tall fresh flower topper designed by the florist.

Like the baker, the photographer proved to be no real problem either. By the time she arrived, the bridesmaids were buzzing around the mirror putting the finishing touches on their hair and makeup, so everyone quickly grouped outside in the perennial garden to take advantage of the amazing weather. Marrying in July is risky business in the Midwest, where humidity levels can turn flowers, dresses and hairdos into limp noodles in a matter of minutes, but Mary had been blessed with brilliant sun, cool breezes and temperatures in the eighties. By the time the pictures were finished in the garden, it was time to leave for the church.

Mary's matron of honor's husband, Brian, had been designated to drive the bride to the church.

"Wow!" he exclaimed when he saw her. "You're the second prettiest bride I've ever seen."

Besides knowing how to deliver a great compliment, Brian proved masterful at ensuring that the bride made an entrance. Because they had to pass the church to get to the parking lot, he stopped the car before they reached it, hopped out and shooed Aaron and his grooms-men inside, so Mary would not be seen alighting onto the circular drive that wrapped around the front of the tan stone church. Aaron, he insisted, must not get so much as a glimpse of his bride until she came down the aisle. The priest further aided the cause by having the bridal party hide in one of the confessionals until everyone was seated.

Like a little girl waiting for the school auditorium to fill up for the third-grade Thanksgiving pageant, Mary peeked through a crack in the door as the guests were escorted to their pews. When the last one slipped in, the bridal party lined up at the doors.

"All the Days of My Life . . ."
Suddenly the prelude music stopped. For the space of a few seconds—silence. And then the first notes rang out from the organ—Pachelbel's Canon in D Minor, the processional she and Aaron had so carefully selected. Mary's heart pounded as the bridesmaids made their way down the long aisle. Already her face hurt from smiling so much, but it was a smile of such deep and genuine pleasure that the pain seemed as joyous as the music, the flowers and crowd. She felt strong, sure and grown up but at the same time curiously childlike to find herself standing at the door of her childhood church holding on to Daddy just as she had so many times before.

Taking a deep breath, she moved resolutely forward, conscious of the bright, misty eyes of dear friends and family watching her from the pews. She could see them, feel their presence, but none of the faces swam into focus except one. It belonged to five-year-old Lea, the daughter of the woman who had been her closest friend at her first professional job at the Mansfield Library.

"Psssst! Lea!" she whispered.

The little girl was so busy gazing around the church she didn't realize that the bride was almost in front of her. Now her mouth dropped open as if to say there was no way this . . . this . . . vision could be her familiar Mary!

Smiling even more broadly, if such a thing were even possible, Mary joined her tall, handsome husband-to-be at the altar.

"You look beautiful," he whispered.

Imperceptibly she nodded. It was true. She did look beautiful, and she knew it in every fiber of her being. It wasn't conceit or any sense of self-glorification that told her this but rather the simple knowledge that any woman so filled with love would have to be beautiful, even if she had not been wearing a dress of lace and walking with her arms filled with flowers.

And then—it seemed like no time at all—she heard the priest say, "Since it is your intention to enter into marriage, join your right hands and declare your consent before God and his church."

Mary turned to Aaron and offered her hand. Firmly she stated, "I, Mary, take you, Aaron, to be my husband. I promise to be true to you in good times and in bad, in sickness and in health. I will love you and honor you all the days of my life."

Aaron looked down into the same wide blue eyes that had stared in astonishment at the green plastic engagement ring he'd offered two years ago this month and repeated just as firmly, "I, Aaron, take you, Mary, to be my wife. I promise to be true to you in good times and in bad, in sickness and in health. I will love you and honor you all the days of my life."

"You have declared your consent before the church," the priest stated. "May the Lord in his goodness strengthen your consent and fill you both with his blessings. What God has joined man must not divide."

They were married! *Married!* Mary squeezed Aaron's hand at the same moment he squeezed hers.

But there was time only for that one brief, private acknowledgment because now it was time to pray. Mary did not think about the party that lay ahead or dwell on the astounding transformation that had just taken place. They were in God's house to give praise and thanks, and that was what they did, actively participating in the singing of the hymns and the repeating of the responses. Only once did she cry. At Communion her eyes blurred with quick tears as she sang the old hymn "Blessed Are They."

Oh yes, blessed indeed were they, these friends and family members gathered here in the sight of God to share this sublime joy. Blessed the little ones like Lea and Aaron's cousins, five-year-old Jack and his little sister Maddie, and two-year old Allesandro who wanted to "dance rock 'n' roll at Mary's wedding!" Blessed her parents, and Aaron's parents. And blessed too her cousin Father Bill Christy, a Spiritan priest and missionary in Tanzania. She had so wanted him to perform their wedding, but he had had to decline. No way could he get home to the United States in July, he'd explained regretfully. But then, miraculously, a conference had cropped up along with the need for surgery on his ankle—and now here he was, serving as Eucharistic minister. It was almost too much joy to contain.

After Communion the final prayers were said. The priest performed the blessing, and the organ began to pound out "City of God." Mary and Aaron swept down the long aisle hand in hand. Out in the bright sun they blinked, as much from astonishment as from the glare. Eight years they had been together. Eight years and now—at last!—they were actually husband and wife.

The rest of the time at the church was a flurry of picture-taking, greeting guests, laughing and exchanging hugs and kisses until finally they were whisked away to dinner at the nearby Conewango Club on the corner of Market and Second. A huge basket of pink geraniums flanked the front door of the brick building with its broad shady porch and thick wide columns. Mary inhaled their spicy fragrance as she brushed past, through the front door and up the three flights of stairs to the party room on the top floor. Everyone was there waiting, and she and Aaron hurried in as though into a warm embrace. The room looked like a garden—crisp white linen cloths with green cloth napkins, the tables graced with bright flowers in terracotta pots, and tall rented trees covered with twinkling white lights. It wasn't formal or fancy, but it was so Mary—bright, perky, casual, and most of all very, very welcoming.

After the introductions and toasts were made, the bride and groom cut the cake but declined to toss either the bouquet or the garter. Mary had no single friends left to catch the former and was repelled by even the suggestion of the latter, however "tastefully" it might be done. But she had had the florist make up a small replica of her wedding bouquet for little Lea, who would carry it proudly down to breakfast the next morning as though a bridal bouquet were the perfect accessory for purple shorts and plastic sunglasses!

After dinner, during which the bridal party and guests intermingled at common tables, Mary and Aaron took to the dance floor alone for "their" song, "You Make Me So Very Happy." Mary and her dad had agreed to forgo the traditional father-daughter dance. Although he was a wonderful dancer, he hated the limelight, and Mary would never ask him to be in it for even a second if it made him uncomfortable. So when he appeared at the second song to dance his one and only dance of the evening with her, she was surprised, delighted and touched.

Mary danced all night. She did the Macarena, the electric slide and even the chicken dance. But then suddenly—too soon—it was 9:30. She and Aaron had a long drive ahead of them to reach the inn at Lake Chautauqua where they would spend the night before heading off on their honeymoon.

"Thank you, ladies and gentlemen, for joining us, and good night," one of the groomsmen announced over the microphone. "We hope you had a wonderful time tonight. We will end the evening right back where we began with 'You Make Me So Very Happy.' "

Once again, Mary and Aaron glided across the polished wood floor together. It was awkward slow-dancing with a height difference of more than a foot, but at this moment, on this day of days, there was no such thing as awkwardness. Just complete and utter joy. So caught up were they in savoring every second of this last dance that at first they didn't realize what was happening. One by one, the guests rose from their chairs and joined them on the dance floor. But instead of breaking into pairs as they had all evening, this time, as if by some unspoken command, they formed a circle. Paul and Helen. The Olsons. Father Bill. The wedding party. Allesandro. Lea. Little Jack and his sister Maddie. Aaron's grandma—everybody—joined hands and began to dance around them.

Mary looked over at the gift table heaped and mounded with packages and white envelopes. She thought of the two lovely showers she'd had—the one her bridesmaids had thrown at the cottage in Chautauqua and the surprise shower her fellow librarians from Medina had given her one Friday night after work. She thought, too, about Tony, the only male librarian on staff, and how he had shelved his discomfort to come along with all those women to the party. Those were the real gifts, not the things that waited in the boxes or envelopes. Of course she would appreciate every one of them, use them, enjoy them, make a home with them, but when she thought back on her wedding day they would not be what she would remember best.

She would remember the flowers growing in her father's garden, the balloon bouquet on the porch, the bridesmaids' breakfast, the look on Lea's face when she saw her in her bridal finery, Aaron telling her she was beautiful, and her dad dancing with her incognito. But most of all she would remember this whirling rainbow circle, because in it she had caught a glimpse of God. And he was dancing too.

Notes

Chapter 1: Lifting the Veil on the "Storybook Wedding"
"While that's enough to strike terror . . .": Marriage Savers Homepage, www.marriagesavers.org/msinfo.htm

"The wedding business in this country is a 35 billion . . .": "Weddings: A $35 Billion Dollar Market," *Target Marketing* 21, no. 5 (May 1998): 66; and Christina F. Watts, "Here Comes the Money: Fashioning a Bridal Consulting Business," *Black Enterprise,* July 1994, p. 29.

"But the event that set the standard . . .": Cecil Woodham-Smith, *Queen Victoria: From Her Birth to the Death of the Prince Consort* (New York: Alfred A. Knopf, 1972), pp. 203-4.

"At a time when the line of demarcation . . .": Michael J. Herr, *Victorian Britain: An Encyclopedia* (New York: Garland, 1988), p. 510; and W. J. Reader, *Life in Victorian England* (New York: G. P. Putnam's, 1964), p. 54.

"Only during the Depression . . .": Meg Cohen, "Goin' to the Chapel?" *Harper's Bazaar,* June 1993, p. 157.

"Ever since, new products and services . . .": Amy Lapinsky, "Taking the Plunge in Style," *St. Paul Magazine,* January 1997, pp. 102-3.

"In 1997 *Bride's* . . .": Erika Isler, "Regional Bride Books Line the Aisle," *Folio: The Magazine for Magazine Management* 24, no. 4 (1995): 22.

"What's interesting about all this is the fact . . .": Muriel L. Whetstone Sims, "What the Bride of the 90's Wants in Her Big Day, Her Man and Her Love Life," *Ebony,* June 1997, pp. 58-60.

"According to industry analysts . . .": Constance C. R. White, "The Price a Woman Pays to Say I Do," *New York Times,* June 27, 1997, sec. E, p. 4.

Chapter 2: Till Debt Do Us Part
"Since couples are older . . .": Carroll Stoner, *Weddings for Grown-ups: Everything You Need to Know to Plan Your Wedding Your Way* (San Francisco: Chronicle, 1993), p. 50.

"Remember, too, that the very retailers . . .": Deirdre McMurdy and Diane Brady, "Banking on Bliss," *Maclean's,* June 28, 1993, pp. 40-42.

"What researchers found is that we . . .": Dan Seligman, "Why More Money Won't Buy You Happiness," *Medical Economics* 74, no. 18 (September 8, 1997): 207-11.

"A second point . . . the Beatles had it right . . .": The song is "Can't Buy Me Love" (John Lennon and Paul McCartney) from the album *A Hard Day's Night,* Capitol Records, 1964.

"As researcher Michael Argyle . . .": Michael Argyle, *The Psychology of Happiness* (London: Methuen, 1987), p. 99.

"Richard A. Easterlin, an economist . . .": Edward Cornish, "Happiness and Wealth," *The Futurist* 31, no. 5 (1997): SR13-16.

"Popular columnist Dave Barry . . .": Quoted in McCurdy and Brady, "Banking on Bliss," p. 40.

Chapter 3: Tradition Or Tyranny?
"The day Victoria Adelaide Mary . . .": Cecil Woodham-Smith, *Queen Victoria: From Her Birth to the Death of the Prince Consort* (New York: Alfred A. Knopf, 1972), p. 388.

"Robert Fulghum, a minister and popular author . . .": Robert Fulghum, *From Beginning to End: The Rituals of Our Lives* (New York: Villard, 1995), p. 113.

Chapter 6: From This Day Forward
"Studies have shown that . . .": Michael G. Lawler, "Doing Marriage Preparation Right: Are Churches Using Their Scarce Resources in the Best Way in This Kind of Family Ministry?" *America,* December 30, 1995, pp. 12-15.

"In 1997 legislatures in at least eleven states . . .": Francine Russo, "Can the Government Prevent Divorce?" *Atlantic Monthly,* October 1997, pp. 28-32.

"Many of today's twentysomething brides and grooms . . .": Lois Smith Brady and Linda J. Murray, "Why Marriage Is Hot Again (Among Women in Their 20s)," *Redbook,* September 1996, pp. 122-27.

"In 1995 the Council on Families in America . . .": Lawler, "Doing Marriage Preparation Right."

"With 87 percent of all marrying couples . . .": Carroll Stoner, *Weddings for*

Grown-ups: Everything You Need to Know to Plan Your Wedding Your Way (San Francisco: Chronicle, 1993), p. 50.

"But some researchers maintain . . .": Russo, "Can the Government Prevent Divorce?"

"One of the largest studies of premarital counseling . . .": Lawler, "Doing Marriage Preparation Right," p. 12.

"One valuable tool in widespread use . . .": Russo, "Can the Government Prevent Divorce?"

"One of the best-known programs . . .": Marriage Savers Homepage, www.marriagesavers.org/msinfo.htm

Chapter 7: Pictures for a Family Album
"But before you start fantasizing . . .": Kimberly Lankford, "Going Abroad to Tie the Knot," *Kiplinger's Personal Finance Magazine,* February 1998, p. 140.

Chapter 8: All Good Gifts
"A case is point is an essay . . .": Charles W. Morton, "Wedding Presents," in *Jubilee: 100 Years of the "Atlantic,"* ed. Edward Weeks and Emily Flint (Boston: Little, Brown, 1957), pp. 224-26.

"Ninety percent of . . .": Leah Ingram, *The Bridal Registry Book* (Chicago: Contemporary Books, 1995), p. 8

"The Federal Housing Administration . . .": Marcia Pledger, "Picking Out Gifts That Count," *Plain Dealer,* June 28, 1998, p. 5H.

"A young Dutch bride . . .": Arlene Hamilton Street, *A Bride's Book of Wedding Traditions* (New York: Hearst, 1995).

"If that sounds shocking . . .": Teresa Riordan, "For the Guests, Giving Made Easier Yet," *New York Times,* May 25, 1998, sec. D, p. 2.

"All Good Gifts," from the Broadway musical *Godspell,* music and lyrics by Stephen Schwartz (New York: Valando Music and New Cadena Music, 1971).

Chapter 9: Let 'Em Eat Cake
"Horst Shulze . . .": Quoted in Martin E. Marty, "Not Much Room at the Inn," *The Christian Century* 111, no. 1 (1998): 39.